GOOD DRAMA!

GOOD DRAMA!

INVITING DRAMATIC

SOLUTIONS TO ELEVATE YOUR

BUSINESS AND YOUR LIFE

Carmen White & Lennie Smith

COPYRIGHT © 2025 CARMEN I. WHITE AND LENNIE A. SMITH
All rights reserved.

GOOD DRAMA!
Inviting Dramatic Solutions to Elevate Your Business and Your Life

FIRST EDITION

ISBN   978-1-5445-4899-9   *Hardcover*
       978-1-5445-4901-9   *Paperback*
       978-1-5445-4900-2   *Ebook*
       978-1-5445-4902-6   *Audiobook*

Library of Congress Control Number: 2025907490

To the undying spark within us that keeps us going against all odds.

CONTENTS

INTRODUCTION 11

1. YOUR GIVEN CIRCUMSTANCES 21
2. YOUR CHARACTER MOTIVATION 47
3. ONE BEAT AT A TIME 67
4. YOUR DRAMATIC CONFLICT 85
5. YOUR SUPPORTING CAST 107
6. SETTING THE STAGE 129
7. ACT AS IF 151

CONCLUSION 173
ACKNOWLEDGEMENTS 177
ABOUT THE AUTHORS 181

"All the world's a stage. And all the men and women merely players."

—WILLIAM SHAKESPEARE

INTRODUCTION

> *"It ain't about how hard you're hit; it's about how you can get hit and keep moving forward."*
> —Sylvester Stallone as Rocky Balboa in *Rocky Balboa*

It was December of 2014. We had just published our first book and were making the rounds on the motivational speaking circuit. We were in the early stages of developing our concept and vision of being Drama Doctors and utilizing Dramatic Solutions to work with companies and individuals to help them grow. Our business was doing so well that we bought a second home, a three-bedroom condominium in a gated community in Florida. We were close to the million-dollar mark in revenue. We had twenty or so people working for us—a combination of full-time employees and independent contractors.

We had been building our business for fifteen years. At the time, our work was focused on drama therapy and expressive arts for adjudicated youth and their families. Additionally, one of our central source contracts focused on workforce development and career coaching for Temporary Assistance for Needy Families (TANF) recipients throughout all eight wards of the District of Columbia.

We had several government contracts, including our anchor contract, which was with the local government and focused on servicing adjudicated young people. Successively, we accrued additional contracts within the metropolitan area. During our developmental years, our "wraparound" within the juvenile justice system was by far the largest contract that we had, and it was what helped our business grow to such a respectable size. We eventually invested in a nice-sized office space, and our children were both in private schools. We spent summers and Christmases with our family at our condominium in Florida; we thought we had it all figured out.

We had no inkling that by early January, most of our contracts would be pulled out from underneath us.

Dr. Lennie had been juggling running our business with his full-time job as a tenured professor and chairman of the fine arts department at a nearby university. As the fall semester came to a close, he was asked not to return the following semester—they had reorganized, and his position was no more. We lost our most significant government contract shortly after, and our anchor became unmoored. The other organizations we had contracts with were smaller contracts, and as word spread that we had lost the first one, these smaller contract holders grew nervous. One by one, they started pulling the plug as well.

Soon, we couldn't pay the rent for our office space, and our landlord filed a lawsuit.

Our world crumbled bit by bit—we couldn't keep our employees working. We took our son out of private school. We sold our car—a fancy black Denali that we drove to CarMax and sold for the somewhat low price of $8,000. We gladly took that money, which helped us survive the next several months. We sold our Florida condo, and when our funds went down to nothing, we even had to put our house in Maryland on the market. The theater went dark, and the story of our lives started to unravel more each day.

We will never forget driving down to the conference in Myrtle Beach to launch our just-published first book. We skimped on meals and used coupons to put gas in the car. We had no other choice at the time but to bring our children. We recall giving them coloring books to use in the conference hallways while we presented. We had a booth at this conference; Dr. Carmen spoke to the crowd, and everyone loved our message and our book. Still, we were so knocked down by the unfortunate turn in our financial situation that we couldn't soak it in. We felt like imposters—how could we stand there and lift all these other people up when we were so low ourselves?

By the end of 2015, life had dealt us a long series of hard hits. The walls had come tumbling down. But because we had such a strong foundation of faith and purpose in our marriage, we knew we would figure something out. We also knew that, somehow, we had to make a tremendous paradigm shift.

We wrote this book to help others understand what we did to turn around and rebuild our lives. We want to help you learn that often what appears to be a failure is an opportunity to recommit to playing out your best role in life. Whether in your business or your personal life, when things take a downturn, you can turn to the Seven Acts we lay out in the book and reset your career and your life so you can play your best role. Getting through tough times is never easy. But if you embark on this journey of using Dramatic Solutions' Seven Acts to elevate your business and your life, you will soon learn that the work is worth the rewards.

In the 2006 movie *Rocky Balboa*, Rocky, now sixty, imparts some wisdom to his son when his son comes to him in protest of the big fight he's got planned against young reigning champion Mason Dixon. Rocky's son has had a hard time building his own identity in the shadow of his father, and he fears his dad's attempt to resurrect his career will make Rocky and his son look bad. That's when Rocky explains to him how hard life hits us all, and with deep conviction, he expresses to his son that it's not about how hard you're hit, it's about how you keep moving forward in spite of those hits.

We started small. A friend of ours who was a clinical psychologist in the public school system, Dr. Denise Daniels, suggested that we think about why we were going through this rough patch. What could we learn from this? What could we avoid in the future? How could we use this as an opportunity to grow? She also suggested we get some contracts with schools, get out there, and teach for a while. We could make decent money and keep our house, she thought.

We thought about what we could learn from what had happened to us, and we realized that, for one thing, we couldn't just rely on one full-time job or one big government contract anymore. We started picking up a few small contracts here and there. Dr. Lennie taught as an adjunct at the same university that demolished his program, which was a humbling experience. He also applied to several other universities, and we both kept knocking on proverbial doors for the business. Eventually, thankfully, we picked up enough of those more minor contracts to be able to keep our house.

At a certain point, we looked at each other and realized that, somehow, we would be OK. Dr. Lennie, in particular, insisted that we just needed to keep doing our entrepreneurial work, go all in on it, and grind. We needed to give it everything we had.

We will never know why this happened to us, but we do know that it ultimately led to us finding our true calling. We decided to make changes that were more aligned with our vision of our work as Drama Doctors. We had been aiming to help others use dramatic solutions to grow in their personal and professional lives, and we began to apply those principles and solutions to ourselves and our own situation.

We began by identifying the good and bad actors in our lives. A handful of people had come through for us. Our children's private school reduced our tuition when they learned about our dire straits. Our accountant reduced his fees, and a friend helped us create a new website for free.

Others weren't as available to help, like healthcare providers who turned us away for lack of funds or colleagues who were in positions to help us but never did. We started to discern between who was in our corner and who was possibly betting against us.

One of our greatest "good actors" was the late Linda Harlee-Harper. She was the director of the Department of Youth Rehabilitation Services in the District of Columbia, and we were awarded a contract with that department for a hundred thousand dollars. This was the beginning of our rebuilding journey. She was the one who also suggested we show strength in our husband-and-wife relationship and allow ourselves to be vulnerable by being transparent about that. We had been afraid of people's perception of us as weaker because we were married. But she helped us see that the opposite was true. As a result, we "came out" as husband and wife, stopped hiding our marriage and seeing it as a detriment, and started celebrating it and allowing it to strengthen our work instead.

The fallout might have harmed or even ended some people's marriages, but because we had nothing when we met and because we had always found something to keep us going in the past, we had our faith in God. We were already married, but our friendship amplified through this period as our choices reaffirmed our shared values and mission in life.

We learned to create space between ourselves and those bad actors. We knew that we could change our model. We took funds from our retirement and invested in a franchise, believing it would give us more security. Through this unsuccessful venture, we learned that we needed to stay true to our calling; we needed to be working in our gift. We needed to keep dreaming big and doing the work instead of abandoning our passion. We started to focus on building our Dramatic Solutions business using our talents and education in drama-based training.

As we set out to relaunch our entrepreneurial journey, we also decided to be more transparent in the community about the fact that we were married. We had kept that quiet during all the years of growing our business and never let on that we were husband and wife and had two amazing children. We didn't want people to think they were getting a two-for-the-price-of-one deal, but we were also simply trying to keep our public identities as professional as possible.

Surprisingly, we realized that once people learned about this, it actually strengthened our image and enhanced our brand. After all, as the Bible tells us in Ecclesiastes 4:9–12, "two are better than one."

We make a great team, so why not lean into that?

We believed, and genuinely lived, the idea that you can't necessarily do or be anything you want, but you can become the best version of yourself, and we became living proof of it. We believe everyone can create their best leading role through knowing and accepting their strengths and weaknesses and working through a series of acts, which we call the Seven Acts to Creating Your Best Role. This is one of the core philosophical components of our company, Dramatic Solutions.

The Seven Acts are: Your Given Circumstances, Your Character Motivation, One Beat at a Time, Your Dramatic Conflict, Your Supporting Cast, Setting the Stage, and Act as If.

The *Oxford English Dictionary* defines "drama" as "an exciting, emotional, or unexpected series of events or circumstances." We have adopted that definition when we talk about drama, especially Good Drama.

We decided to write this book so that you can better understand what we did to turn around and rebuild our lives to develop personally and professionally and, hopefully, see how you can do it, too. We want to help you learn that what appears to be a failure is often an opportunity to recommit to playing out your best role in life. Whether in your business or your personal life, when things take a downturn, there are steps you can take to motivate yourself and build your career back up. To be emphatically clear, seeing yourself through that perceived rough patch is indeed trying and will test you, yet it is not only tolerable and doable but also valuable.

When we first set out to write a book about using seven critical acts of drama to reset, restory, and rebuild your life, it was partly because of what we see all too often in our trainings, workshops, seminars, church, and with friends. Over the years, we've counseled thousands of people who have reached some level of success in their careers but are stuck in many other ways. If this sounds familiar, then this book is for you.

Many people have lost their passion and excitement for their jobs and feel stressed and unhappy. They've started overeating, drinking too much, smoking, or engaging in any number of self-destructive behaviors because of the anxiety they feel. Their fuse has gotten shorter, and they're overwhelmed with the demands of constantly troubleshooting issues at work and at home.

People are increasingly bringing their work home instead of delegating it and maintaining a work–life balance. As a result, they're experiencing more physical pain, like migraines or back and neck pain, because their emotional pain has manifested in their bodies. In the acclaimed book *The Body Keeps the Score: Brain, Mind, and Body in the Healing of Trauma* by Bessel van der Kolk, MD, the author recognizes that the power of the body to absorb and reflect back to us our thoughts and feelings is truly amazing.

In the modern economy, it's often difficult for people to get to a place where they can own their own home. Many people must continue to rent for years on end, and frequently, they yearn to be in a relationship but haven't found that special someone yet.

We decided to write this book to reach more people experiencing these things, people with an urgency to reset their lives and a readiness to embark on a new way of thinking about human and professional development. This new way of thinking has its roots in a drama-based perspective.

Suppose you're ready to grow personally, working to gain a promotion or rebrand professionally. We invite you to elevate your life with the Seven Acts in your back pocket. The Seven Acts have their origin in the theater because, if you think about it, what we see on a stage is just a reflection of ourselves in the mirror. Just as watching actors perform in a play gives us a glimpse of how characters can learn, heal, and grow, you will find that using the seven dramatic acts in this book will help you learn, heal, and grow so that you can make positive changes in your own life and create your starring role and develop your given talents.

We believe that if you apply the Seven Acts, you can have a reset in your thoughts and start to discover and amplify new habits, get away from your old habits, and acknowledge how trauma has played a role in your leadership, your communication skills, or your quest to find and sustain healthy, happy relationships.

We invite you to do some self-reflection as you read these pages. You will find that we have presented tangible actions and methods that will help you see yourself walking down a pathway of success, help you take concrete actions to reset your thinking and being, and help you live your success story, gaining valuable wisdom throughout the journey.

This isn't so much about being OK with what is happening around you but about being OK with yourself. Whether you're not making as much money as you want, hate your job, or long to be in a relationship, being aware of these things is the first step toward growth. For actual change, of course, you have to take it further.

In this book, we will show you how to make your vision of success in life a reality by working on yourself in specific ways. We will also show you how to use these simple yet critical strategies to grow in your personal and professional life instead of staying stuck.

To do this, you'll be empowered to:

- Acknowledge and accept Your Given Circumstances
- Discover Your Character Motivation
- Make positive changes One Beat at a Time
- Better handle Your Dramatic Conflict
- Choose Your Supporting Cast wisely
- Prepare for success by Setting the Stage
- Act "as if" to embody your best role

Each of the Seven Acts will be explored in detail on the pages of this book, with examples of how our clients put them into practice. We will also show you how we used the Seven Acts to materialize a great marriage and partnership, financial and physical health, and a thriving business. We will share more details of the disastrous crisis we endured in our business some years ago and how we used these Seven Acts to rebuild our company and our lives. As a result, we have reaped the success we dreamed of, and now we want to help you do the same.

ACT ONE

YOUR GIVEN CIRCUMSTANCES

"It's not your fault."
—Robin Williams as Sean in *Good Will Hunting*

In 2014, we specialized in drama therapy and conflict resolution through drama services for adjudicated young people and their families. Our anchor contract was with the District of Columbia. At the time, we were both board-certified drama therapists helping youth who were serving time in juvenile facilities.

Many of these incarcerated youth were serving short sentences for small crimes, but we were also dealing with some high-end young criminals who had received "juvenile life." That means that they would be there for a very long time, with the possibility of having to go into an adult facility when they become adults and serve life in prison. At this time, our work was evolving, and we had started training others to use our approach as well. We expanded our client base and started helping adults, going into youth group homes and working all over the city, helping what the government calls "special populations."

That year, we coined a new term for ourselves: Dramatic Engagers. We both attended New York University (NYU) and had similar backgrounds in theater and educational theater. We started developing theatrical exercises based on Konstantin Stanislavski's school of thought and the thoughts of other leaders in acting theory and creative drama strategies. We took the liberty of evolving them to make them a little bit more culturally competent and psychoeducational because we needed to target a different type of person. These were people who had committed crimes and needed to be rehabilitated, not actors preparing for a role.

Using these and other principles, we devised our own method of training and personal development for incarcerated youth, and one aspect of it involved the concept of Your Given Circumstances.

When working with this specific population of young people, the idea of owning your past—understanding, defining, and accepting your physicality, your conflicts, your motivations, and your relationships—became a turning point in their lives and ours. You can imagine some of the backgrounds they had survived. For example, at one point, Dr. Lennie was working with a group of young men who had grown up in the same neighborhood he did. Dr. Lennie made the mistake one time of saying something to one of the young men along the lines of, "I grew up here, man; I know what you're going through." Dr. Lennie felt like he knew how hard it was for them and what they'd had to do to get through each day.

The young man grew quiet and said, "No, you don't know what I went through."

Dr. Lennie insisted, "Yes, I do. I grew up in the same neighborhood as you."

And the young man said, "Well, did your mother leave you in a trash can? No. So how could you say your experience is the same as my experience?"

Dr. Lennie will never forget that; it changed him. He learned a lesson that day: Just because you have the same physicality and made some bad decisions growing up in the same neighborhood, it doesn't mean you have the same story as someone else. Everyone has their own story. Many of the histories of these young people is very dark, and we were asking them to confront and accept their past experiences, which were often filled with unbearable traumas.

The adolescents we sometimes worked with had suffered challenges beyond the scope of what most people endure throughout their whole lives. But over the years, we found that helping them, and all of our clients, define, accept, and even embrace their given circumstances was a powerfully effective way to help them begin to heal and reset their lives. We realized that understanding their given circumstances helped them make better choices—ones that were healthier for them and those around them.

In December 2014, we had just released our book and were ready to take it on the road for a book tour to sell copies. We were in Florida for some downtime over the holidays, staying in our condominium there. We had just signed a contract for ten thousand dollars to pay a company to help us build capacity in our business and, in particular, to acquire federal contracts. We had no idea that every single one of our state and local contracts was about to be pulled out from under us the next month.

The reason for the crisis was complex. It was partly because our business practices needed improvement, and we had not set ourselves up with enough multiple contracts. There were a few bad actors involved as well, which we will cover in more detail in Act Five, Your Supporting Cast. For now, for several different reasons, one by one, our contracts were pulled. This didn't happen because of any bad actions on our part; sometimes, you can do everything in your power to make things work, but things can still go wrong. Besides, DC is a small town in many ways, and so there was also a bit of a domino effect involved that helped topple our business.

We also discovered that we were the only entrepreneurs in our families and that we were dealing with insecurities, impostor syndromes, traumas, and financial management challenges that we had experienced in our lives, and that we needed to deal with.

Whatever the reasons, those events led to our hitting bottom financially and needing to find a way to reset and reboot our lives.

Those events became our given circumstances.

IN ACTING

In the theater, when an actor takes a role, they have to research the character. They need to look at the script to do that, and from the information there, they can create a past story for the character. This is what allows them to get "in character" and remain in character and really connect with who they're going to play on the stage.

Actors sometimes create a storyboard for their characters. They chart what schools they attended and what jobs they had, think up milestone experiences they had, and create a whole backstory to that character's life, even though it's not in the script.

In the theater, identifying past experiences is part of doing your homework. It is looking at what other characters are saying about you and identifying how your character deals with certain things. It's like you're creating a story for the actor to prepare for, and it really helps you with the authenticity and power of your performance.

In acting, this is called discovering Your Given Circumstances.

Konstantin Stanislavski, who coined the term, was considered the father of modern acting. As he designed it in his system, the first step is to read the script and analyze the character you will be playing to identify their background, relationships, beliefs, desires, and motivations. Actors also look to discover the societal contexts of culture and history in which their character exists. Simply put, it's defining and describing the who, what, where, when, why, and how of your character. This helps the actor play the role in the most authentic and compelling way possible.

In this process, the actor is looking at interior circumstances, such as shyness or a big ego, and external circumstances, such as their parents' income, the food they eat, and the area they live in.

START WITH YOUR BACKSTORY

We use drama as a tool for personal and professional growth. Because we use it in our personal lives and we use it in our professional lives, we know that creating your best role in life is, first of all, understanding your historic traumas and embracing them. We all have a backstory that we can't change. You may have to do some research to understand where that backstory came from, but your backstory makes you who you are today. Because of those situations, traumas, and experiences in your past, there are going to be times when you have emotions you will have to deal with.

The first step on the journey toward resetting and elevating your life is to acknowledge what is hindering you from being your best self. We do this first by making a thorough assessment of our background and our past experiences.

EMBRACE YOUR STORY

Understanding and accepting Your Given Circumstances is about embracing your story. This allows you to focus on recognizing the importance of leaning into your story in a way that permeates internally. This means you really soak it up. You take it all in and connect with your story. You connect to the feelings that come up for you when you begin to take the actual steps of taking a deep dive into the details of the events of your past.

Embracing your story is one of the biggest steps you'll ever take in life because your story is the strongest asset you'll ever have. As you consider how you want to be perceived in the world, it's important to identify the values you hold for yourself. This reflection enables you to think about how you navigate both your personal and professional life. Everyone's story is unique, so start by identifying the key players in your narrative and reflecting on how your story has evolved over time.

For instance, during the first seven years of your development, think about who wrote your story. Who directed it? Who acted as the producer? Consider the main characters of your story: the stage manager who supported you, your mentors, coaches, best friends, and loved ones. Reflect on the roles these individuals played in your life and how they influenced you emotionally, socially, spiritually, and economically.

Take a moment to acknowledge the impact these characters have had on your life. How have they evolved? Are they still part of your journey?

Additionally, consider if there are characters in your life you need to let go of—those who may hold you back from embracing your full story, especially those who have caused you harm or trauma, whether intentionally or unintentionally. Was it a specific situation or an unexpected turn of events that shaped your experiences? Reflecting on these aspects can help you better understand your narrative and the lessons learned along the way.

Embracing your story requires honest and sometimes difficult self-reflection, but if you want to prepare for your best role in life, it's where you start.

Actors often will create a storyboard of their character's life and make choices about who they are and what makes them that way, especially in terms of their motivations. For an actor to truly prepare to embody the role, sometimes they must not just embrace that story but also "restory it."

RESTORY YOUR STORY

Restorying is a multifaceted therapeutic process involving gathering and analyzing an individual's personal narratives. These stories are deconstructed into key elements, such as time, place, plot, and scene. Through this deep exploration, clients are encouraged to identify and examine the underlying themes and patterns that may be shaping their current perceptions and behaviors.

According to the article "Narrative Research: A Comparison of Two Restorying Data Analysis Approaches" by Ollerenshaw and Creswell, "Restorying is the process of gathering stories, analyzing them for key elements of the story (e.g., time, place, plot, and scene), and then rewriting the story to place it within a chronological sequence as clients explore their experiences to find alterations to their story or make a whole new one."[1]

When we get stuck and forget our lines, actors just say, "Line," and someone else feeds them their line. But when we get stuck in life, we can have the autonomy to rewrite our scripts rather than seek answers about our next move from an external source. This is another way to look at restorying.

To embrace your story is to acknowledge and accept Your Given Circumstances: physicality, conflicts, motivations, and relationships. It means you own your story and are the writer of your own script. Don't sit back and let someone else feed you your lines!

In the October 2020 *Psychology Today* blog post, "Why Examining Your Past Is the Best Way to a Better Future," the author states, "Once you've cleared up the history, you own your destiny."[2] We believe this is the heart of it all.

Another way to examine Your Given Circumstances is to think about what other people in your life might think about you. What are your patterns and cycles? What has plagued your life in some way?

Your issue might be alcohol, or it might be violence or abandonment in your past that caused trauma in your life.

We all have stories, and sometimes, it seems like our scripts are already written once we get to a certain point in our lives. We can't ignore the things that have occurred, the things that have happened to us, or the things we've done in the past. But we can find opportunities to rewrite our scripts to match new objectives we might have in life.

---

[1] Ollerenshaw, JA, and John W. Creswell. "Narrative Research: A Comparison of Two Restorying Data Analysis Approaches." *Qualitative Inquiry* 8, no. 3 (2002): 329–347. https://doi.org/10.1177/10778004008003008.

[2] "Why Examining Your Past Is the Best Way to a Better Future." *Psychology Today*, October 2020. https://www.psychologytoday.com/us/blog/dysfunction-interrupted/202010/why-examining-your-past-is-the-best-way-to-a-better-future/amp.

Dr. Lennie, for instance, can't shy away from the fact that there was alcoholism in his household growing up. That is his given circumstance. Dr. Carmen was adopted at a very young age into a happy, loving home, but her biological mother suffered tragic abuse at the hands of her husband. This is a part of Dr. Carmen's given circumstances. Our collective given circumstances also included being raised by two loving parents who were rooted in Christian principles, which they modeled and raised us both to live by. We both are appreciative that our given circumstances consisted of an upbringing that stressed the importance of education and what it meant to be kind to others.

How do we embrace our given circumstances, reflect on our past experiences and our past stories, and use that information to understand what makes us who we are? For instance, Dr. Lennie doesn't drink now because of how alcohol was abused in his family. He has been able to reflect on his past and embrace his story so that he can learn from it and not make the same mistakes his family made. He has restored into his new story of playing his best role as a person who doesn't drink.

Doing an inventory of Your Given Circumstances not only involves being analytical and critical but also hopeful because, through acceptance and acknowledgment of your past, you can move on and create a better future.

Actors are taught that there are three parts to the concept of Your Given Circumstance: a character sketch, which is our story; a physicality, such as being only four foot eleven even though you may want to be six foot two; and the conflict—that which is in opposition to a character's motivation. If you're working on your character as an actor, you're looking at the script to identify parts of the character sketch.

As an actor, you need to think about your physical descriptions and identify the conflicts within and outside yourself, your motivations, and the relationships you inherited or are going to acquire as the story unfolds. For instance, you entered this world with a family; that is a given. And then, you had the opportunity to create new relationships and build friendships. Some were healthy relationships, and others may have been unhealthy relationships.

Another thing we do as actors is read our script to analyze what other characters around us think of us. What are they saying about us? How do they act around us?

We realize most of our readers are not actors, and this book is about creating your best role in real life. The point is, you can use these techniques in real life just as easily. Think deeply about Your Given Circumstances—your physicality, your relationships, the conflicts in your life, and your motivations. Pay attention to how people react to you, talk about you, and communicate with you.

Actors also identify patterns and cycles in the life of the character they are going to play. In Dr. Lennie's personal story, alcohol had been in his family for a long time. There was a pattern of alcoholism and violence. At the cookouts and the funerals and all the family gatherings, drinking was always a problem in his family, and they eventually turned to fights and violence. Dr. Lennie identified his family's cycles and patterns, and this helped him see the larger forces at work rather than just focusing on certain individuals.

Whatever traumatic things may have happened to you in your past, especially in those early childhood years up until age seven, you need to become aware of them and mindful of how they might be plaguing your life to this day. As Carl Jung is credited with saying, "Until you make the unconscious conscious, it will rule your life, and you will call it fate."

Let's say you look at your past, your story, and you just want to forget about it. You just want to let it go, and so you "Act as If" that can magically happen. You can try that, but in reality, your past is not going anywhere. There are scars that will always be there.

This is not going to be easy work. In the film *Good Will Hunting*, Robin Williams's character, Sean, who is Will Hunting's therapist, repeats, "It's not your fault" ten times, saying it more forcefully each time until Will finally breaks down and realizes that the abuse he suffered as a kid was out of his control. This is because, for so many people, being traumatized causes us to question what we must have done to cause the bad things to happen to us. As illogical as it seems, it's human nature to feel unworthy and unlovable because of what was done to us by someone else.

You may not want to revisit those memories. They may have been traumatic and disturbing. Why should we embrace and love the bad things that happen to us? Simply because that's how we can find compassion, self-love, and forgiveness. It's how we can let go of shame, guilt, and feelings of low self-worth. If you want to think of it as acknowledging instead of loving, by all means, go ahead. The term we have adopted for it is to restory your story. That is what is done in the theater and in therapy.

For instance, at age seven, Carmen found out that she had been adopted and lived for quite some time not knowing why her birth parents had given her up. She went for many years not telling anyone that she didn't tell people that she was adopted. Ultimately, she restoried her story and was able to gain perspective on it enough to know that it was nothing to be ashamed of or to hide.

The goal is to acknowledge and integrate your past and Your Given Circumstances into your whole life. Analyze those things and become aware of the key elements, whether they are good or bad.

The ultimate goal of restorying is to empower clients to reconstruct their narratives in a way that fosters a greater sense of agency and self-understanding. This may involve identifying and challenging limiting beliefs, reframing past experiences, and envisioning new possibilities for the future. By actively participating in the reauthoring of their own stories, clients can develop a more coherent and empowering sense of self, leading to increased well-being and a greater capacity for change.

In essence, restorying serves as a bridge between the past, present, and future, allowing individuals to integrate their experiences into a cohesive and meaningful narrative. This process facilitates the exploration and reinterpretation of personal experiences, ultimately leading to the creation of a new story that is both authentic and empowering.

CELEBRATE YOUR STRENGTHS

We have been focusing so far on the difficult and traumatic parts of our lives, but what about the positive aspects and elements of our past? These can also be embraced so that you can become more aware of your strengths and opportunities. We met each other in New York City at the American Musical and Dramatic Academy (AMDA), where we were both actors in training. We both succeeded in academia at New York University, and we have built a beautiful relationship and family life. Yes, our business fell apart in 2014, and it took several years to recover, but we have created a whole new business, a much stronger and more resilient one at that. This is the very essence of Good Drama.

It's about being bold in the things you ask God for. From a spiritual base, you are embracing your story where it shines and restorying the story about the times when things weren't so great. The good moments both play against and for the past.

Dr. Carmen, for instance, has been restorying her story since she was a child. She was adopted shortly after her birth, and she owns that informed trauma. She grew up in an extremely healthy household. It was very loving. Her adoptive parents were empowering forces in her life. However, her siblings, who were also adopted out, did not grow up in the healthiest of homes.

Since Dr. Carmen had a stable mother, educational opportunities, and much more, she could create a new story for herself, a much more positive one than perhaps what her siblings, who lived very different lives, could identify with. It's important to pause and reflect on what happened to you that gave rise to positive things and created goodness in your life. Dr. Carmen ended up being the first in her biological family to graduate from college, for instance.

It is crucial to understand that embracing the good in your past can help you improve your behavior, moods, outlook on life, and how you treat others.

WHAT GENERATION ARE YOU?

Another factor to consider about yourself is your generation. When we conduct diversity training, we are helping people of all ages and generations understand each other better and get along. Sometimes communication is a struggle since different people were born during different eras and have different perspectives. One of our trainers, for example, was working with a group of teenage clients. A young man in the group, for some reason, asked her to call him Da-Dae. She came to us, and she clearly had a big problem. "I am not calling him that. That is not professional."

Dr. Lennie said to her, "Look, you have to realize, when we were young, we went to work nine to five and we dressed a certain way, but now the new generation is coming to work in a T-shirt and getting paid to play video games. The environment has changed. You need to look past your own experiences and focus on the overall goal to connect with this young man and then hopefully move him forward." The generational identity is another helpful way to examine and put into perspective your own Given Circumstances as well as the circumstances of other people.

In the theater, we do a lot of research. We identify the past experiences of the character either through research, learning, what other people say, or what we create. In real life, to embrace that is to accept it fully and welcome it into your reality. For actors as well as nonactors, embracing also means loving your whole story, the good and the bad.

WHY DO THE WORK

When Cory Hawkins played Dr. Dre in the film *Straight Outta Compton,* the actor says he spent a lot of time with Dr. Dre, both off and on the set.[3] He wanted to play the whole man, so he tried to learn everything about him. When we look at not just what makes us different

---

3   Gray, F. Gary, director. *Straight Outta Compton.* Universal Pictures, 2015.

but also those commonalities we have with others, we understand their whole selves. Only then could Cory restory Dr. Dre's story in his own way and portray the character through the unique lens of his research. Looking at the ways in which we are like many of the humans around us is another way to identify our given circumstances.

The fundamental meaning and purpose of our given circumstances is this: We want to look back and understand our whole past so that we can avoid making the same mistakes and instead intentionally keep building on our strengths. We are integrating our stories instead of pushing them away, burying them, or denying them. We are reframing those pieces of our story that might be getting in the way of our endeavors in the here and now.

As part of this work, we can also examine what we learned from our parents. Dr. Carmen learned the value of working hard from her father, and Dr. Lennie learned the same thing from his father, who never missed a day of work.

This is probably why, when the business crashed in 2015, Dr. Lennie considered taking a nine-to-five job just to get back in the workforce. But it's also most likely why we both decided to stay on the entrepreneurial path, which certainly involves hard work. We had a dream, and we were determined to pursue it.

OUR STORIES

As husband and wife, we have been working with our given circumstances to help our marriage grow in many ways over the years. Part of the work involves understanding ourselves as individuals, and part of it involves our relationship with each other and how this affects the dynamics between us at times.

Dr. Carmen, much more than Dr. Lennie, was supported as a child in extracurricular activities. She was able to pursue dance and acting, and her parents took her to all sorts of cultural events. Dr. Lennie went to the movies a lot as a kid. When we first met, Dr. Carmen didn't even know what going to a movie was like—she was so busy always performing and doing other activities. But now, we both love taking our kids to the movies.

Dr. Lennie didn't have that. His father couldn't afford to give him those opportunities for extracurricular activities, and in fact, his father grew up not even knowing his own father, so there were many challenges for both Dr. Lennie and his father growing up.

When Dr. Lennie wanted to go to college as a young man, he told his father about his dreams, but at that time, his dad was going through a difficult divorce with his mother. His father confessed that he couldn't help Dr. Lennie, and he suggested that Dr. Lennie go into the military and use the GI Bill benefit to pay for school after serving his duty. This suggestion was rooted in his father's father's given circumstances because for Black males during his time, the military was the only way to make a life for oneself. These days, looking back, Dr. Lennie can see that this reaction from his father was because of his father's reality and his father's circumstances, and not a message to Dr. Lennie or a reflection of his father's love.

Dr. Carmen's story, her given circumstances, seemed so comfortable and supportive as her childhood and young adulthood unfolded. Her parents stayed together; she was very well cared for and lived a middle-class life on a cul-de-sac in the suburbs just outside of DC.

On the other hand, Dr. Lennie and his brothers and sisters spent more time tearing each other down than building each other up, and this also affected him. Out of seven brothers and sisters, he was the first one to go to college. However, he remembers his grandmother vividly saying, "Find a good girl who wants something in life."

When he met Dr. Carmen, he quickly learned that she grew up with big dreams and wanted so much. She was determined to live a lifestyle that he wasn't used to. Dr. Lennie remembers talking to his father and telling him that Dr. Carmen went and got her hair and nails done at least once a month. His father told him that he should be thankful that he has a girl who likes to take care of herself. This helped Dr. Lennie gain perspective, but he wasn't sure that he could step up to the plate and be all that she might need him to be. Growing up the way he did had an impact on his self-esteem. Because of this, as an adult, sometimes he didn't see himself as a high achiever. But at a certain point, he realized he could let that low self-worth go and restory his ambition to align more with his present-day circumstances. As a result, he was able to step up to the plate.

Examinations of our past should be focused on clarifying why and where you were given limiting messages that are now holding you back. Ask yourself questions like, *Where did you get your first idea that you weren't as good as everyone else? When did you first get the idea that the world is a scary place filled with things you can't handle? Where did you get these negative messages from?*

Dr. Lennie, for instance, is less outspoken about many things than Dr. Carmen. When something happens to him that he doesn't especially like, he's more inclined to just let it go. He doesn't understand why she bothers with it sometimes. For instance, if they're in a restaurant and their food gets delivered cold, Dr. Carmen is going to ask the waitress to fix it. Dr. Lennie would rather just live with it. This comes from his past experiences and the ways his mother and father dealt with things.

Negative messages contribute to the things we fear in life, how we deal with our finances, and so many other things in our lives. Acknowledging and accepting Your Given Circumstances requires first digging for them and making sure we are even aware of these things that drive us. And then we have to accept them and even embrace them.

Going back to acting, once you do your research, it should motivate how you behave and act. Once you are able to identify those given circumstances, you can move forward toward exploring some of the decisions you've been making and try to pursue other actions that have more positive outcomes.

Dr. Lennie is now aware that when his food comes back cold, it's OK to mention it and ask the server to warm it up. He is not going to be mean about it, but just assert that he's dissatisfied instead of letting the negative messages in his mind prevent him from having a warm plate of dinner. This isn't about beating yourself up over your reactions. It's about giving yourself grace now that you have a better understanding of the reasons behind the reactions that you have.

For us, it's about recovery, rebounding, and restoration. It's about repairing any harm that you did to yourself and repairing the harm that you've done to others. That kind of rebound will allow you to create a new pathway as you clean out the weeds.

WHEN OUR PAST JOINS OUR PRESENT

When our business was shattered and the company went into a serious decline, we were scrambling, both personally and professionally. We felt strongly that we needed to keep the family close together. We had a deep desire to make sure that our kids still had food and shelter and the basics of life, but also that they still felt loved and didn't lose their sense of joy or their sense of being children. We fought hard to make sure our kids still had nice things and experiences in their lives. Much of that truly came from Dr. Carmen's past because, even though she was adopted, she had two loving parents and all the niceties.

Dr. Carmen is deeply appreciative and grateful for her adoptive parents and the life they gave her. And the truth is, her trajectory could have been extremely different. This became evident when she learned that her biological mother and her stepsiblings had dramatically different pathways.

During the rebound of our company, we also moved through a rebound period for our family, and this involved examining our own pasts. We started talking more about embracing our stories in our work with clients, and we made efforts to learn more about our own history at the same time.

Dr. Lennie decided he wanted to find out who his grandfather was since his father had never known, and Dr. Carmen really knew nothing about her biological family. To begin our journeys, we started with Ancestry.com. Just a little spit in the cup started it all.

First, Dr. Carmen found a cousin who looked similar to her through Ancestry.com. We were traveling back home from Florida on a train when she discovered this relative. Dr. Lennie reached out to this cousin and told her about Dr. Carmen, and told her we wanted to know how she was connected to Dr. Carmen. This young lady called back, and after we talked with her for a while, she said, "I think I know who your mother is. Let me call you back."

And then someone else, an aunt, called us back and said, "Yes, I know who your mother was."

From this exchange, a connection was formed between Dr. Carmen and members of her family who knew all about what had happened to Dr. Carmen's mother, her stepbrother, and sisters. Dr. Carmen learned that the only reason her mother gave her up for adoption was that she herself was a victim of domestic violence. When Dr. Carmen's mother and her husband were splitting up, he shot Dr. Carmen's biological mother seven times—at the dinner table. Her husband was upset with her because she had had a relationship with someone else and, hence, had become pregnant by someone else. This means her mother was most likely carrying Dr. Carmen in her womb at the time.

During Dr. Carmen's biological mother's process of healing and also of deciding to carry and give birth to the baby rather than have an abortion, her two uncles moved her away from Florida to Washington, DC. This way, her mother could carry the baby to term as far away from the man who was trying to kill her as possible. Dr. Carmen's adoptive parents had experienced the tragic loss of a stillborn baby and adopted Dr. Carmen in a sealed adoption about six months after she was born. Dr. Carmen's biological mother remained in the Washington, DC, metropolitan area and later worked as a surgical technician.

Apparently, one of Dr. Carmen's sisters witnessed the shooting of her mother. This sister nursed their mom back to health. When she met Dr. Carmen, she told her something along the lines of, "You have no idea how bad it was. It's amazing you survived. You were really meant to be here."

When we learned about this less than ten years ago, Dr. Carmen had no idea that her birth mother had been living in the DC area all these years and raising three other children. When she did learn this, she was told that her stepbrother and stepsisters had experienced some serious challenges. Certain stories she was told had been passed down through the family. Her stepbrother, according to the stories, had gotten into quite a lot of trouble. All of her biological siblings were said to have experienced challenging times, but the most extreme tragedy was that Dr. Carmen's stepbrother eventually ended up killing Dr. Carmen's biological mother, according to the news.

As horrible as this is, it can be explained by his given circumstances—his father had been violent against his mother, so it became more likely that he would do the same.

The murder made national headlines. Dr. Carmen even remembers reading about it in the news at the time it happened, but of course, at that point, she had no idea that the story was about her own biological mother.

Before this, Dr. Carmen had never pursued knowing anything about her history. Somehow, she had heard that someone in her birth family was in jail, but that was it. But after learning all this, we went down to Florida and met the whole family at a restaurant. Now, years later, we remain connected, and Dr. Carmen has been able to visit her mother's grave site.

Most people don't even know Dr. Carmen was adopted. She doesn't talk about it or share it. We're pretty sure a lot of people reading this book will be surprised by it. But Dr. Carmen is glad she learned all of this in 2018 when our business was on the rise again. This news was the cherry on top of the sundae. In the work we do for underserved communities, specifically women suffering from domestic violence, this experience has deepened her ability to really connect with those women.

It's also possible that Dr. Carmen's chosen career was a way of unconsciously honoring her biological mother. She always wanted to help African American men of color who were incarcerated. In fact, her thesis at NYU for her master's degree was on the consequences of gun violence in inner-city communities. And that was many, many years before she knew about any of the violence in her own past. Because of both of their given circumstances with domestic violence, they created a foundation to help kids in college who are adopted or who have experienced domestic violence.

Dr. Carmen is still processing her own story. For example, she knows that had things gone differently, and she hadn't been adopted into the family she was in, she would still be a dancer, still deeply connected to music and the stage, but the dancing would have likely been on somebody's pole in a strip club. It would not have been the safest stage, but she believes she would have taken it anyway because performance is in her DNA.

In truth, many of our present circumstances have been triggered and informed by our pasts, especially in early childhood, and whether we are conscious of what happened or not, we need to find acceptance for who we are every step of the way.

Had she known the truths about her past, Dr. Carmen may have unconsciously held herself back and not felt as empowered. This is a clear example of how knowing and understanding our given circumstances can have such a transformative effect on us. When there is horrible trauma in our past, if we don't deal with it properly, examine it from all sides, and restory it, it will hold us back and impair our confidence and sense of self-worth.

SOUL WORK

If you look at our stories, you might think we were victims. But when you restory our stories, you can see that we are both survivors, not victims. We carry trauma from all that happened, yes, but we also carry wisdom about life that not many people have. As we work to acknowledge the trauma and deal with it, we are creating a reset and a renewal.

This is about accepting who we are. It's what we call soul work.

Allow the pain to be the pain and the hurt to be the hurt because it will come out one way or another. If you don't go deep and do the heavy work, then you will never know when your past is going to creep up on you and get in the way of your ability to play your best role in life.

Don't shy away from your past. Use it! That way, you won't make the mistakes of your past again in your future.

The work of reflection for many of us isn't one of trauma, but for some, it is. And so it might not be a reflection of pain, despair, or hurt that weighs us down. It might be a reflection of overcoming joy. It might be time for you to feel a level of gratitude as you reflect on your past, the good and the bad.

You need to understand this so that you can prepare yourself for an even greater future.

There are some specific ways that we approach this in our work, and we believe this has been some of our best work. We used to work with adults who were either resetting their careers or hadn't really gotten them going as they wanted due to life circumstances, obstacles, lack of education, or lack of employment.

This had caused them to become stuck in their momentum to reach their financial or household goals. Part of the program involved creating what we called life tapestries. During the building of these tapestries, we asked some critical questions.

The level of inquiry would take them back to the first seven years of their lives, and we were very specific about that time frame. Why? Because every seven years, our makeup changes. The cells in our body regenerate, and this new makeup brings different experiences and perspectives. In our work, our questions remain the same for each aspect of life—years one to seven, seven to fourteen, fourteen to twenty-one, etc.

In each of those time frames, we ask our clients what their obstacles were and what their accomplishments were. What worked? What didn't work? What were your stressors and your relationships? Our clients use words, pictures, and graphics to create their tapestry. Some people want to draw symbols; others want text. We give them stickers, magazine articles, and newspaper clippings, and by the end, they've created a beautiful mosaic.

For some, the process itself is cathartic, just putting it all together into this beautiful art form. But for others, it is not truly cathartic until they can affirm their experiences by verbalizing why they put what they did in their life tapestry, why they placed certain things where they did, and how they answered the questions.

These are adults who sometimes come off as tough-skinned, poised, and very conservative, and we know they are thinking, *You're not going to get me to cry*. However, once they engage in this process, it becomes a very therapeutic experience. They unpack certain memories in their lives and examine the messages in their heads. Almost always, there are no dry eyes in those rooms.

We often want to separate our personal persona from our professional identity, but we've learned that they mirror one another. There's a connection; those who are healthy in their personal lives tend to be some of the most outstanding leaders. It's not always the case, but we've noticed that when people are happy at home, they seem to be happy at work as well.

We're not talking about superficial happiness; we're referring to a deeper contentment. When leaders feel supported and go back to acknowledge their past—how their "table" was set up—they can often realize what pieces are missing. This awareness enables them to seek the support they need, redefine their goals, or reach out to new mentors and work on their own growth as humans.

Everyone needs an anchor and desires support. They need a buffer to process their thoughts and see where they can improve. The life tapestries and the mask work are two examples of how the work we do guides people, helping them to see their lives through a new lens while also supporting them to begin to think about certain mechanisms that they need to not repeat bad habits and sharpen the things that work well for them.

We have learned the value of accepting who we are. We have

also learned to value the work of becoming people we can continue to accept and embrace. We've been married for almost thirty years, but when one of us says something or does something, and we don't like what we said or did, we reflect on our backstory and realize maybe that was the way our father or mother used to talk to their spouse, but we can do better. We want to create a much healthier way of being in a marriage, but if we hadn't come to understand our backstory and become clear on our given circumstances, we wouldn't even know anything was wrong or that we could change the culture of our relationship.

During the rebuilding of our business, as part of our rebranding, we began to refer to ourselves as Drama Doctors. During our sessions, participants now call us Dr. Carmen and Dr. Lennie.

As Drama Doctors, we believe that you can be anything that your God-given talents allow you to be in your life. You can play your very best role in life every day if you do the work to acknowledge what's getting in your way.

To return to the jargon of theater, now that you have acknowledged Your Given Circumstances, you can do the internal work from the inside out to be able to interact with the rest of the world. In your own life, you are the director as well as the actor, so you get to figure out your own blocking and write your own script. Which way do I go now? This type of question is usually best answered by you, not someone else, and the crucial first step to finding answers is to discover your motivations.

CREATE YOUR BEST ROLE

Act One: Your Given Circumstances

This activity is similar to creating your own personalized vision board. However, vision boards tend to focus on future projections, whereas Life Tapestries focus on acknowledging past experiences and present situations to create future projections.

1. Gather any or all of the following materials before starting this exercise:

    a. Cardboard or construction paper
    b. Scissors
    c. Glue sticks or tape
    d. Colored markers or colored pencils
    e. Pencils and crayons
    f. Magazines and newspapers
    g. Cards and photographs

2. Using colors and words from your materials and imagination, start to answer the questions one by one. Allow yourself to start cutting out pieces of newspaper, magazines, cards, and pictures that ultimately reflect your answer to the following prompts.

The Questions:

1. What were you exposed to when you were growing up, especially between ages one to seven? Consider your demographic area, your family members and their communication styles, your education, what you did for recreation, the smells, food, and other sensory input from your childhood, etc.
2. What are your accomplishments?
3. What were some challenges that you overcame? Try to identify two or three.
4. Where will you be in the next five years?

Now, review your resource materials and paint a picture that reflects your responses to the individual questions.

Keep in mind that you're focusing on your past when answering the questions. The first question is the only one that pertains to the first seven years of life, and the last question is the only one that makes a projection about your future.

Now, start to organize and design your life tapestry based on Your Given Circumstances.

As you progress through the exercise, be mindful of your breath. Where do you feel your breath is strongest? Where do you hold it? How does it feel going in and out of your body? Remember to breathe throughout this entire process.

Once you have completed the life tapestry and answered all four questions, take a picture of it.

This activity will help you monitor and assess your own personal values as they pertain to past experiences in relation to Your Given Circumstances, particularly those things that you had no control over, as well as the choices you made when encountering Your Given Circumstances.

Note: We recommend that you find a journal, open a document on your computer, record a memo on your phone, or use other means to capture your inner thoughts and reflections after doing the activities and visualizations at the back of each chapter in this book.

This is a way to process your past, present, and future in real time. It will provide a way for you to process the information. It will help you acknowledge your own filter, process your emotions, and evaluate your opinions as you dissect the material.

ACT TWO

YOUR CHARACTER MOTIVATION

"I had lost the ability to bullshit. It was the me I'd always wanted to be."
—Tom Cruise as Jerry in *Jerry Maguire*

Many things happened during the period of 2015 and 2016 during our struggles to rebuild and recover, and in the process, we rediscovered the value of getting clear on our motivations. Of course, what had been important to us in 2014 wasn't as relevant in 2015 because, at that time, we had really lost everything.

We had to reset and focus on basic motivational factors: living, eating, paying the grocery bill, keeping the lights and water on, keeping a roof over our heads, and ensuring our kids were safe, healthy, and educated. It was a dramatic shift back to basics. It made us reassess and prioritize in a very practical way.

We were also dealing with how hurt and broken we felt coming out of that unexpected financial downfall. Dr. Lennie was especially bitter about the loss of his job; it felt so unfair, and it triggered old emotions of low self-worth for him. Commitment and loyalty are important to him, and he felt like he was letting his students down. He was deeply disappointed, and we both felt rejected.

One of our motivations that didn't change was our commitment to enjoying life and doing things that made us happy. We used coupons and found deals wherever we could. We packed up and took the kids to the beach one day—just drove down to Ocean City and had a wonderful time as a family. It was what we could afford at the time, but it turned out to be one of the best beach days we've ever had. We had a fantastic time. The kids didn't know we were broke—they were too young to realize. They just knew we said "no" to certain things, and they didn't question why.

That same summer, despite not having much money, we stood in long lines to get half-price tickets for Broadway shows. We stayed in New Jersey and took the bus into New York City to see the show. Our daughter was turning twelve, and we wanted to make it special for her. We saw *Spider-Man: Turn Off the Dark* and were literally in the last seats in the house, way up top, where you feel like you might fall into the orchestra pit if you move around too much. The show ended so late that the bus stopped a mile from our hotel, and we had to run through a neighborhood alley to get to our hotel. Our daughter will never let us forget that day!

But we made it happen. These small, joyful moments during tough times have stuck with us and created lasting, meaningful memories.

IN ACTING

In Lee Strasberg's method acting, which is based on Stanislavski's system, actors prepare for their role through techniques to raise their awareness of the emotional life of the character as well as their motivation. They ask, "What does my character want?" and "What actions can I take to achieve my objectives?"

This deep analysis of their goals and desires helps them determine why the character is in this story and why they are essential to it. Actors contemplate how they will achieve their characters' goals, what is driving them, and how achieving their goals will change them. They also explore how the characters interact with each other and whether one character's wants and needs might impact or intersect with another character's wants and needs. All of these are investigated on a physical, mental, and emotional level.

WHY FIND YOUR "WHY"

Simon Sinek, organizational leadership expert and author of the books *Start with Why* and *Find Your Why*, asserts that we all have a "why" for the things we strive for. At Dramatic Solutions, we believe that if you want to play your best role in life, you first need to get clear on what you want and why you want those things. Why is it important to find your "why"? If you are aware of your deeper motivations, it helps you make better choices, choices more aligned with what you want and need.

For example, we are both currently very focused on our health. Why? Because we want to be around for our grandchildren. We want to be able to play with them, run with them, and enjoy them to the fullest. Knowing this helps Dr. Lennie get up early and go to the gym, and Dr. Carmen attends a yoga or Jazzercize class.

This book is about playing your best role, living your best life, and choosing your best work. It's all about being your best self. And that all starts with your "why." Why do you want to get that promotion? Why do you want that better house or that degree? Do you know why? If you clarify your "why," you're getting clear on where you want to go and who you want to be.

Examining our "why" helps us recognize what's in it for us. When we forget the benefits or reasons for our actions, our "why" serves as a reminder of the reason we embarked on that journey in the first place. It helps guide our path, even when things go wrong or when others get in the way of our goals.

When we keep our "why" at the forefront of our efforts and actions, it governs our behavior, attitude, and character. This, in turn, allows us to not only attract positivity but also draw in people who will support and encourage us to stay the course. Even when we stumble, these people can help us get back on track.

What is motivation? Motivation is the internal process that drives an individual to take action toward achieving a goal or completing a task. It is what energizes people, gives them direction, and sustains their efforts over time.

One of Dr. Carmen's favorite acting professors, Professor Mitchell Hébert from the University of Maryland, helped her learn how great actors approach their scene work by teaching the concept of the three levels of motivation: Either you want something, you need it, or you must have it.

THREE LEVELS OF MOTIVATION

Categorizing your goals into these levels can clarify your priorities. For example:

- Want: A desire, like wanting to take a vacation.
- Need: A necessity, such as having a stable income.
- Must-have: A nonnegotiable, like protecting your family's well-being.

Understanding where your goals fall on this spectrum allows you to focus your energy on what truly matters.

If we merely want something, the energy we invest may be minimal. If we need it, our focus sharpens. But when it's something we must have, we're fully committed—nothing will stop us from achieving it.

While this concept definitely helps our clients in their personal and professional lives, we also adopted it as a crucial tool in our own lives. If we look at the three levels of motivation during 2015 when our business had failed, it wasn't about wants or even needs for us—it was about "must-haves." We had to survive.

The three levels can also help when we're in conflict. If you find yourself getting into a fight with someone, you can ask: Is it worth it? Do I just want this win, or do I need this win? Is it a must-have? This framework also helps us decide on the level of time we invest in things. How much thinking will be required, and how much analysis do we have to undertake here? It can also help us create a plan of action or decide how much money we're willing to spend on something. For instance, do we want to spend five hundred dollars on a certificate program, or would reading the summary on their website suffice? Understanding our motivation helps us make choices about virtually every aspect of our lives.

We've learned that we had choices regarding motivation and that we could give ourselves a little grace if we didn't achieve everything we wanted at a particular time. Maybe we didn't have all the tools or the capacity at that moment to accomplish one of our goals. Perhaps our motivation factors were disrupted or interrupted. Sometimes, these things take more time than we anticipate.

DIFFERENT MOTIVATIONS, DIFFERENT SITUATIONS

Our motivations also shift as we go through different phases in life. Life stages bring changes, and with them come different priorities and motivations.

In our own lives, we've used these concepts to rebuild during challenging times. For example, in 2015, when we lost nearly everything, we reevaluated our goals and shifted our approach. We realized that having just one contract wasn't sustainable, so we set financial goals that included diversifying our income streams.

Right now, we're focused on getting healthy and staying that way. Our motivation is to be able to play with our grandkids and to spend as much time as possible doing our work as Drama Doctors and enjoying life together. These are powerful motivations!

For others, these shifts happen for various reasons: death, divorce, debt, demotion, or even positive changes like getting married, having a baby, or winning the lottery.

When motivations shift, it's important to let go of certain things to make room for newness while still preserving what worked for you in the past. It's about nourishing what helped you grow and making room for fresh opportunities.

VALUES AND OUR "WHY"

In the District of Columbia, like many large cities, we face challenges such as violence and loss. Lately, the city has struggled with a heartbreaking number of shootings and murders, many involving young African American males. Some of the violence is accidental, some intentional, but all of it serves as a reminder of why we do the work we do. We do it because we both greatly value helping others.

Our "why" connects to our values. Taking inventory of our values can help us apply our "why" in everyday life. For example, if we value self-expression, we might journal, write, or communicate more with our families. If we value creativity, we might create an artistic space in our home and make time to paint, draw, write, or play music.

In our sessions, we often begin by inviting participants to explore their values. Whether working with a corporate team, school, nonprofit, or government agency, setting norms at the start helps us move forward collectively. We encourage people to honor, acknowledge, and accept their own values as well as the values of others to create a productive and inclusive learning environment.

Values don't just define our motivations—they also govern our actions. Values and motivations are interdependent; they're cyclical. Our values help us stay on track, align our actions with our motivations, and keep us grounded.

When we help people identify their values, we usually share examples. For us, faith is a big one. Faith represents a belief in something beyond ourselves—a belief in the unseen and the unknown. Another value is forgiveness. We aren't perfect, and neither are others. Prioritizing forgiveness allows us to grow, heal, and move forward.

A third value for us is authenticity. We place a high priority on being genuine and truthful. We often talk about how dishonesty, lack of trust, and artificiality pull people away from their motivations. Being aware of what aligns with and detracts from your values is critical.

Motivations are deeply personal and individual. Whether intrinsic or extrinsic, motivation drives us to act in alignment with who we are, and since everyone is different, we all have varying motivations. If we're not aware of this, it can lead to conflict, and in fact, in drama, the source of most conflict is the opposing motivations of the characters. It can also make life interesting.

For instance, Dr. Lennie often jokes, even at the worst times, because humor is intrinsic to his personality, and he values joy. Dr. Carmen, on the other hand, is more motivated by nurturing and appreciation.

It's also important to reflect on how negative self-talk or unhealthy habits can erode our motivation. Recognizing these patterns and staying true to what truly motivates us helps us take corrective action and get our actions in line with our values.

Dr. Carmen often shares her story as a mother of two miracle babies. These experiences have profoundly shaped her motivations. Our first child was born prematurely at one pound fifteen ounces, and our second child was born one month early; the doctor had to engage in a high-risk emergency delivery. Both experiences were life-threatening but ended in miracles. Today, when Dr. Carmen looks at our children, she feels deeply motivated and grounded.

Ultimately, understanding motivations and values allows us to live authentically, rise to life's challenges, and create more meaning in our personal and professional lives.

This is an opportunity to ask yourself questions like: *Is it worth being in a toxic or unhealthy relationship with my mother-in-law? She's likely going to be a part of my life for a long time, so how do I maneuver that relationship? Where does it fall on my spectrum of motivations to fix or repair it?*

INTRINSIC AND EXTRINSIC MOTIVATIONS

Motivations can be either intrinsic or extrinsic. Intrinsic motivators are just what you'd think—they're internal—like a passion for creativity or a desire for self-improvement. Internal motivation comes from within the individual—driven by personal values, enjoyment, passion, or a sense of purpose. An example might be a team member in your organization who works hard on a project because they enjoy the challenge and the opportunity to learn.

Extrinsic motivators come from external sources, such as financial rewards, recognition, or avoiding consequences. An example of this might be a team member who is motivated to complete a project to earn a bonus or get praise from their manager.

Intrinsic motivations are the things you've been naturally drawn to since childhood. When we're unsure of our path or questioning our decisions, going back to those core desires can help us navigate scary changes or big decisions.

It's the intrinsic motivations, those values and passions we've always had, that keep us on track. They help us identify what drives us naturally, regardless of external rewards.

Extrinsic motivations, like money or recognition, can help, but if we focus too much on them, we risk losing sight of who we really are. We might take a job for the money but later realize it didn't make us happy. That's OK—it's part of the journey. At some point, though, we need to return to our true selves and reconnect with what brings us joy beyond materialistic rewards.

PSYCHOLOGICAL NEEDS

Intrinsic motivations are often connected to our psychological needs. Let's say you're not getting your needs met or aren't even able to identify your needs. For example, one area of Dr. Lennie's psychological needs is that he is very conscientious, values-oriented, and community-oriented. When he watches the news, he often gets stressed out because of everything happening in the world. He might get upset later that same evening about something totally unrelated. He knows he needs to catch himself and ask himself what he's really upset about. Is it just a scratch in the paint, or is it an unjust war that he just learned about on the news?

If you know things such as this about yourself and know what you need psychologically, you can stay aware and sensitive to it and notice when you might be reacting to something that does not align with your psychological needs. You can choose, in Dr. Lennie's case, not to watch so much news that you get overwhelmed by it. Or you can choose to find someone to talk to about the news in order to express, acknowledge, and accept your feelings so they don't ruin the rest of your day.

Psychological needs are mental or emotional needs that are important for mental health and healthy development. They can be generated internally or through interactions with the environment.

Examples of psychological needs identified by the *Journal of Personality and Social Psychology* include:[4]

1. Autonomy
2. Competence
3. Relatedness
4. Self-actualization/meaning
5. Physical thriving
6. Pleasure/stimulation
7. Money/luxury
8. Security

---

[4] Sheldon, Kennon M., Andrew J. Elliot, Youngmee Kim, and Tim Kasser. "What Is Satisfying About Satisfying Events? Testing 10 Candidate Psychological Needs." *Journal of Personality and Social Psychology* 80, no. 2 (2001): 325-339. doi:10.1037//0022-3514.80.2.325.

9. Self-esteem
10. Popularity/influence

We would also add several other needs to the list:

11. Social approval: Wanting to be accepted by others
12. Justice: Wanting fairness
13. Alone time: Some people need a lot of solitude
14. The courage to take risks: This is often situational, meaning every character we play in life can handle different levels of risk.
15. Job satisfaction: Wanting to be content at work, outside of financial need
16. Stimulation: We want to be challenged through work that sharpens our cognitive skills.
17. Belonging: We want to be around people with similar values, judgment, belief systems, and opinions.
18. Independence: Some like to work independently and don't want to deal with a lot of people.
19. Play: Wanting to free our inner child and just play
20. Physical contact: Where appropriate and with mutual consent

Fulfilling these basic needs is so critical because these are the most difficult ones that we struggle with, especially at work.

Psychological needs are similar to physiological needs, such as hunger, thirst, and sleep. If these needs aren't met, it can affect your well-being.

Our psychological needs are what we need to survive emotionally from an internal perspective. Things like our sense of belonging, self-regulation, and sense of safety are psychological needs. These are based on and very much connected to the three lenses through which we view the world: thinking, feeling, and doing. How much our primary psychological needs are being met will often be perceived through thoughts, emotions, or actions. No matter the type, understanding our motivations requires mindfulness.

We can also identify whether a motivation is a micro motivation or a macro motivation. Micro motivations are the small, everyday things—like wanting a parking spot close to the store or deciding what to eat for lunch. Macro motivations, on the other hand, are larger goals that define our long-term dreams—like becoming a CEO, earning a degree, or retiring in a dream location.

As Drama Doctors, we help people focus on both intrinsic and extrinsic motivations. However, we find that people generally need to work more on rediscovering their intrinsic desires. For instance, when we work with educators, we help them reconnect with why they became teachers or administrators in the schools, especially when the work becomes overwhelming.

We often work with professionals to remind them why they pursued their dream careers, even when those careers turn out to be more challenging than anticipated. We also help many who feel stuck in their current job and need to make a change. Remembering their original "why" can be the key to pushing through the obstacles of change and being resilient through those obstacles.

For actors, this process of discovering their character's motivations teaches them to examine the intentions and inner thoughts of the role. They look at their word choices, actions, and objectives to uncover the deeper motivations behind a role. Similarly, in real life, once we identify our overarching goal, we can outline these nuanced elements of that goal and figure out steps to get there.

In our work, we often help equip leaders with tools and techniques to recognize and nurture their own motivations. We ask them to identify the different types and levels of motivation, and we help them develop strategies to keep both themselves and their teams engaged, focused, and driven to achieve their goals.

MOTIVATION EQUATION AND EXPECTANCY THEORY

Another way to think about and assess motivation within yourself and others is to test it with Victor Vroom's Expectancy Theory. According to this theory, motivation is a function of three factors:

1. Expectancy: The belief that effort will lead to performance
2. Instrumentality: The belief that performance will lead to a reward
3. Valence: The value the individual places on the reward

In Vroom's view, leaders can boost motivation by addressing these three components:

1. Clarify expectations (what's required to succeed).
2. Ensure fair and meaningful rewards for good performance.
3. Make the reward valuable to the individual.

Motivation shapes every aspect of our lives, from the goals we set to the actions we take to achieve them. For some, it's about leaving a legacy or ensuring financial independence for their children. For others, it's about finding joy and meaning in the little things. Whatever the motivation, understanding your "why" makes all the difference.

Motivation, whether intrinsic or extrinsic, micro or macro, shapes our choices and outcomes. By understanding and prioritizing these forces, we can align our actions with our core values and live more authentically.

HOW LEADERS CAN MOTIVATE THEMSELVES

If you are in a position of leadership, you'll need to work on your own motivation as well as be sensitive to your team members' motivations. Self-motivation is key for a leader since you are expected to lead by example. If you aren't motivated, it can be difficult to inspire motivation in others. Understanding your own motivational drivers is the first step toward building a motivated, high-performing team.

Here are some actionable tips for self-motivation:

1. Set clear goals: Create specific, measurable goals that align with your personal and professional vision. These goals should be meaningful and aligned with your values to keep you engaged.
2. Find purpose: Understand the "why" behind your actions. Leaders who have a clear sense of purpose and connection can be more influential and more able to "move" their team members to be motivated to perform at their highest potential.
3. Celebrate small wins: Acknowledge your progress toward larger goals, and take time to reflect on your accomplishments. This will help sustain motivation during challenging times.
4. Maintain balance: Self-care, including physical exercise, mindfulness, and taking breaks, is essential for long-term motivation. Burnout can quickly sap motivation, so it's important to recharge regularly.

Here are some motivational questions that actors use. They can open your mind and invite your brain to think deeply about your hidden and crystal-clear wants and desires:

- What character do you dream of playing, and why?
- How can your unique experiences enrich your performances?
- What is one skill you are currently developing to enhance your acting?
- How do you overcome self-doubt during the audition process?
- What inspires you to continue pursuing acting despite the challenges?
- Which role do you believe would best showcase your range as an actor?
- What is your personal definition of success as an actor?
- How do you plan to stay creatively engaged when facing setbacks?
- What steps can you take today to move closer to your goals?

Here are some more questions to ask yourself:

- What motivates me as a leader?
- How do I stay motivated during setbacks or tough times?
- What are some intrinsic and extrinsic factors that keep me energized and focused?

WHAT WOULD YOU JUMP FOR?

Knowing your true motivation helps you understand your choices, sometimes in dramatic ways.

As an example of this, we often recall a powerful story from years ago when we were involved in selling Excel Communications products and attended a conference in Texas where we witnessed a presentation by a very engaging salesman.

The presenter, who seemed highly motivated, spoke on motivation and expressed how critical it is to discover what drives us. He began with a vivid metaphor. He asked us to imagine we were standing at the top of a towering building, the height of the Washington Monument, with a five-foot gap between us and the next building over.

He asked the audience, "If I placed a million dollars on the other side, would you jump across for it?"

Most of us thought, *Five feet? Sure, we'd do it.*

Then, he made the scenario more challenging. "Now," he said, "imagine the gap is twenty feet, with strong winds blowing. I'll raise the reward to five million dollars—would you still jump?"

Some hesitated. "What about ten million dollars?" Still, many of us doubted if we'd take the risk.

Finally, he said, "Now imagine your son or daughter is dangling on the edge of the opposite building. Would you jump to save them?"

Without hesitation, nearly everyone said yes.

That moment has stayed with us. It was a profound lesson about motivation—what we're genuinely willing to take risks for and why we get up every day to do what we do. It's about understanding what drives us to act with passion, courage, and faith.

At the time, we were sales consultants, and the presentation was meant to encourage us to tap into our motivations to sign more people up for the phone systems we were selling. But the message was much more profound than just sales. It challenged us to get into the right headspace, to connect with what's important, and to continuously pursue our goals with clarity and purpose.

This isn't just about self-improvement—it's also about inspiring others. As leaders, we've learned to channel our motivations to help guide those around us, whether it's our team, staff, or community. Leadership is about understanding what drives people and helping them align with shared goals. It becomes a collective motivation toward a collective transformation. Discovering and embracing your motivation is not always just a personal act—it's a powerful tool for change, both for yourself and those around you.

YOUR INNER VOICE

Sometimes, discovering your motivation requires silencing that inner voice or letting go of the inner child who holds on to past negativity. For example, maybe someone was told by their parents they would never amount to anything. This is why we also need to confront the inner voice that can try to hold us back. Developing a mindful awareness of your self-talk is critical. When it's encouraging, it can fuel your motivation. But when it's negative—when it questions your worth or capability—you need to counteract it by affirming your purpose and value.

Simply looking in the mirror and telling yourself, "I am capable, I am loved, I am ready for the challenges ahead," can reframe your mindset. It's about choosing a constructive dialogue with yourself to drown out negativity and replace it with clarity about where you're going.

DISCOVERING YOUR MOTIVATION

How can you get clear on your motivations? Start by asking yourself these questions:

- What is my "why"?
- What are my internal and external motivations?
- Are these motivations macro (big-picture goals) or micro (everyday actions)?
- Are they wants, needs, or must-haves?
- Why do I want what I want?

Motivation is more than a driving force—it's a guide for making decisions, from leaving a job to pursuing a passion. It informs your abilities, sustains your happiness, and anchors you during challenging times. It's your North Star, helping you stay aligned with your purpose.

A FRAMEWORK FOR LIFE

When we clarify our motivation, we create a framework for continuous growth. It's about accepting who we are today while striving for who we want to be tomorrow. As the film *Jerry Maguire* demonstrated, material things always become secondary to intangible values like love, integrity, and purpose.

Just like the quote from the film, motivation is deeply tied to authenticity. When we align our goals with our true selves—rather than societal expectations or superficial desires—we unlock the potential for genuine happiness and fulfillment.

This process of identifying our goals and motivations helped us prioritize what really matters. For example, when we were finally back up on our feet enough to start looking for a second home, instead of focusing on buying in a specific area, we simplified our goal: We just wanted a place near the beach. Breaking goals into achievable objectives helped us take actionable steps toward making them a reality. This is the subject of the next chapter, "Act Three: One Beat at a Time."

CREATE YOUR BEST ROLE

Act Two: Your Character Motivation

Let's dive deeper into exploring and defining Your Character Motivation. As a reminder, there are two types (intrinsic and extrinsic) and three levels (want, need, and must-have) of motivations.

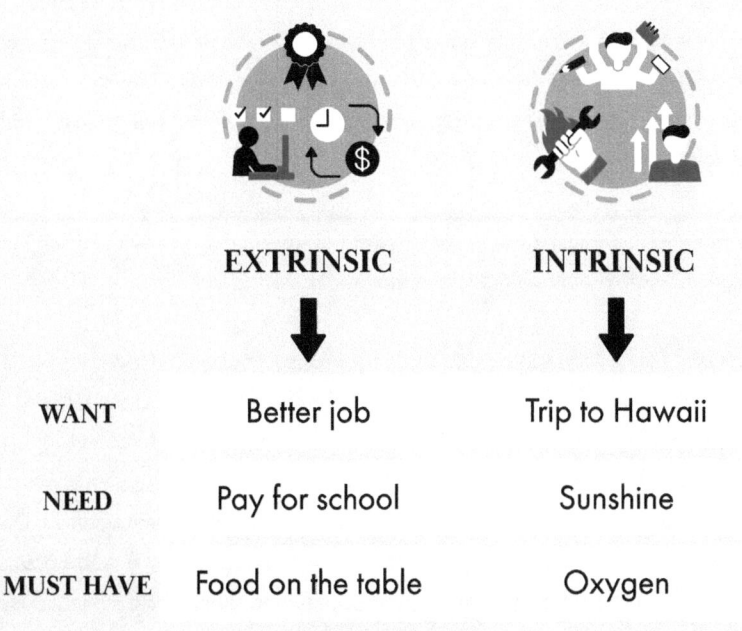

	EXTRINSIC ⬇	INTRINSIC ⬇
WANT	Better job	Trip to Hawaii
NEED	Pay for school	Sunshine
MUST HAVE	Food on the table	Oxygen

Infographic of Internal/External and Want/Need/Must-Have

Here are some exercises that we have used in our trainings and other programs:

Before starting this discovery exercise, find a comfortable chair to sit in and prepare your brain to take in information. Open to the physical parts of your body by breathing deeply and letting go of stress. Continue to take big breaths in and out and brace yourself for that negative self-talk that may hinder your growth, understanding, and healing process. Whatever comes up, let it go.

While you're taking your deep breaths, say to yourself, "I am OK. I am OK. I am OK."

As we move into this motivational walk and talk, keep in mind that this may be a stretch for you. However, keep in mind that the brain is fully nurtured and alive when movement is connected to thought patterns.

Think about a specific professional or personal goal that you have in mind at this given time. Ask yourself, *Is this something that I want? Is it something that I need? Or is it something that I must have?* Once you have identified which motivational effort level your goal falls into, let's move into our motivational walk-and-talk exercise.

Keeping your primary goal in the forefront of your mind, slowly rise from the chair and walk around in the space that you're in.

Think of a few strategies you can use to approach your goal. However, while you're walking and talking to yourself, you want to be able to discover why it is important that you reach this goal.

Be very honest with yourself as you walk and talk things out with yourself. Do you want this thing, person, or situation in your life because you are energized by your intrinsic motivations, or is your desire fueled by extrinsic motivations? Is it that you need this thing to happen in your life right now because of some material gain or because of a human interconnectedness gain? Be deeply, unapologetically, and authentically honest with yourself about what you are identifying with right now.

Continue breathing deeply. Breathe in, breathe out. Now, start to think of and name all the things that will come out of reaching this goal. What are the consequences? What are the benefits of reaching this goal? Take a deep breath and let it out. Take a seat back in your chair and reflect on your experience.

Using your memo app, document, or journal, reflect on your motivational walk and talk. Did you notice times when you were smiling or when your breath started to change? Did you start to feel anxiety around a thought, opinion, or feeling? Were there moments during your motivational walk and talk when you started to tense up? Was there an ease to your body flow? Did you notice how your walk changed? Did you notice your voice tones changing? All these things are indicators to be aware of as you identify your own personal and professional desires to accomplish that given goal.

An optional opportunity is to journal those experiences and to reinstate the identity of what is motivating you to move into completing and accomplishing your next goal in life.

ACT THREE

ONE BEAT AT A TIME

"Great men are not born great; they grow great."
—Marlon Brando as Vito Corleone in *The Godfather*

When we opened our franchise in 2015 with the franchise staffing company Staffing for Us, we quickly learned that the company was heavily focused on cold calls. They gave us clear instructions: We had to make fifty cold calls a day. They outlined early on that our staffing business's purpose was to make these cold calls to get clients. Naturally, we did not enjoy making those cold calls. People were saying mean things to us and hanging up on us all day long. Dr. Lennie hated it, and Dr. Carmen hated it even more, especially since she was the one who had to go out and knock on people's doors.

But some positives came out of it. Staffing for Us was very clear that to be successful, there were small things that needed to be done, and that they would add up in time. They even had a system in place that showed them at the end of the month how many calls we'd made, and we had to let them know how many times we went out and knocked on doors. The accountability factor that came out of that was crucial to them and a great learning opportunity for us.

The system that counted our calls allowed them to generate a report showing the number of calls each of their franchises had made and correlated it with the number of clients recruited. These reports showed that the successful franchises were successful because they followed this specific protocol of calling fifty clients daily.

For us, as owners of a franchise, our overall goal was to get new clients. But in the process, we discovered that to do that, we had to do it One Beat at a Time, one call at a time. This became obvious through the counting of the calls and the reports. This is an example of Act Three: One Beat at a Time, which we now use as a fundamental principle in our work as Drama Doctors.

We were initially unsuccessful in the franchise, and we have since realized that this was because we weren't motivated to be successful in that industry. We weren't living in our gift. We don't even believe in the concept of a staffing agency without preparing people to do the work! Our life's work is conducting trainings to help employees communicate with each other more effectively and deal with conflict better. But at the time, we were using it as a safety net, and the lessons learned about incremental movement toward a specific goal were worthwhile, regardless of how little those actions connected to our motivations.

IN ACTING

In acting, a beat is a moment of change within a scene. It can also be thought of as a shift in mood or tone or a character's reaction to something that changes the trajectory of their actions.

While studying as actors, we learned early on about the power of beat changes. We knew that, for one thing, we didn't have to stay stuck in making one choice repeatedly when we were on the stage. We were free to keep changing our choices. This increased our acting skills and deepened our craft. We were motivated to study our craft even more. We realized we didn't have to keep the same beat for the whole script. We could change and grow and move in different directions until we found out what really worked best.

Stanislavski developed this concept and technique in the early twentieth century, and like much of his work, it was later adopted and expanded on by Lee Strasberg. The important thing is to see that the small steps, the subtle changes we make in life, really matter. You can use the power of beat changes to redefine your next step or create a very strategic plan of action that will help you protect your future. The idea is not to overstep the transactional experience of each moment. This is also about being in the moment. It all comes down to living in the moment—in the theater and in life. This is mindfulness, and One Beat at a Time requires mindfulness.

When you are thinking beat by beat on the stage, you're completely in the moment. You're not preoccupied with either the past or the future. You're in this moment, your moment, and it gives you ownership over your own experiences without comparing your actions to those of the others around you. It also opens you up to being inspired by others.

This is why it's so important to understand your "why" and Your Character Motivation before you begin working toward your goals, One Beat at a Time. The idea is that small steps lead to your end result. But you have to really want that end result. Otherwise, why take even the tiniest step? If the goals and objectives aren't aligned with your "why," and the beats you are taking aren't in line with your motivation, why bother?

But if the goal really speaks to your inner fire, your passion, your needs, and your must-haves, then the path toward achievement is to take it One Beat at a Time. What are the small things you can do that will move you forward? What small changes in your choices and habits can you make?

The power of beat changes lies in the ways it can direct our lives toward our goals, in that moment-by-moment awareness of ourselves as ever-changing and ever-growing. The good, the bad, and the indifferent are all within our authentic experience.

Great actors understand the power of the beat change for this reason: They understand they're living in the moment, especially if they genuinely did their homework around creating a beat change and planned it out to align it with their character's motivation. Even though it may be a similar beat that they are repeating from an earlier scene, the same situation with the same person, they have the chance to live the beat differently. Every day is a new performance.

Anytime the mood or tone of a scene shifts or the characters react to something that prompts them to alter their trajectory, that's a beat change.

It starts with setting concrete objectives to keep you pointed toward your "why." Once that's done, you break it down into One Beat at a Time. Perhaps your motivation is to work in a field where you can help others; that's your "why." As a result, you decide you want to become a nurse. To get there, you'll need to get a degree. Start with researching options for degrees, and you have completed a beat change.

It might be something as simple as reading an entire book. You need to take it one chapter at a time. Think of it as chunking your life. Sometimes, we have to chunk our changes down to just the next hour or even the next thirty minutes.

Beat changes are those moments in acting and in life where you switch to a new thought or a new action to keep everything moving forward. It's about making choices after you've figured out your motivation, choices that will move you forward to your "why." What choices will you make that will drive your thoughts, your actions, and your behavior to support your motivation?

You might decide you want to lose twenty pounds. Obviously, you can't lose it all at once. You need to make small choices, all day, every day, chunking your life to move you toward your goal. Let's say you decide you want to live in a foreign country. What are some things you need to do to your life to chunk it in such a way that you'll be able to make that move?

Dr. Lennie's example is that if he wants to work out and be healthier, he needs to get up earlier so he can work out.

Another way that making changes One Beat at a Time can help you achieve your goals is that since it's all about small changes, if you mess up one day and have that piece of cake, there's always the next day to get back on track and stay there. You don't have to be so hard on yourself for small slips in actions around your goal.

You don't have to run a marathon; just take a walk! You don't have to finish a whole course this month. Just try to do two units. If you want to go back to school, just take one class. Don't get upset with yourself over the lack of perfection or the seemingly smallness of each day's beat change because, in reality, each day's beat change isn't small at all. It's a small but necessary piece of the larger endeavor you've established as having so much meaning in your life.

If you're just starting out in life, you might be overwhelmed by how to find your direction, decide what you want to be, and achieve the necessary degree or training for it. Don't worry about all that; just keep trying until you find the things that get you the results you want.

Don Corleone says, "Great men are not born great; they grow great" in the film *The Godfather* because he knows that true greatness is not something one is inherently born with. It is achieved through experience, hard work, and deliberate choices made consistently every day. This means that no matter your circumstances, you can improve and become great through incremental changes. Life is continuous learning, and success is the result of taking action toward your goal over and over again.

In our world, so many people are dealing with anxiety. They worry about what they don't have, how to get it, and so on. The idea of One Beat at a Time establishes a mindset where you can stop feeling overwhelmed or that you have to accomplish everything right away.

Thoughts, behaviors, and actions. These are the central changes you'll need to make. Even in your thinking process, you need to make changes. As far as your thinking patterns, how can you lay things out to accomplish your objectives at a reasonable pace? Eventually, you will get there. What are the mindfulness activities you are doing in your life? How are you finding ways to relax? Are you getting enough sleep? If you are motivated and looking to become your best role, what new choices could you make?

People who are conscientious, trusting of their choices, and confident in their decision-making will take the time to experience the response to the beat changes they make in their lives. They'll be patient with the responses of their body and their mind to the beat change. This is going to help them be more informed about what the next beat change should be in their life.

The work of actors is to pretend to be someone else. You can try this in your own life when asking yourself what choice you should make at any given time. What would Martin Luther King Jr. do? What would Albert Einstein say? What kinds of choices do great people make that make them great? In Dr. Lennie's view, for instance, Seth Curry is the greatest basketball player out there. Every morning, he goes out and shoots a hundred times from one single spot. He takes time to pray with his family every day, too.

What's significant about these well-known players in the game of life is that each one of them was willing to sacrifice by making difficult choices. In other words, each beat of life is representative of a unit of life, just like characters playing out each objective within a given scene. Your character knows that in order to be fully successful, they must be willing to examine, object to, and evaluate a plan of action, which is generated out of one's individual units in the living aspects of life. This is salient because oftentimes, we make assumptions that either our supervisor, partner, or someone else is expected to provide us with our script, with clear goals and a strategic plan for how to accomplish the multiple goals that we need to achieve.

Interestingly enough, what's missing is how you move from one moment to the next, which is the workmanship that appears clear when you strategically start to outline each beat, one at a time. This informs you of the actual action steps needed to pursue your goals. Even if your goal is to be mindful and at peace, it must still include intentional action behind every unit of life.

Second, we can be lifted up by the rigor and discipline of Dr. King, Einstein, Curry, and others like them. All of them were willing to make tough decisions as they evolved. Much of your reflection and work is going to be in identifying what your beats are, how you want to play them out, and what might be the consequences of your actions when you have fully executed the action step.

Everyone's beat changes are different. Depending on your goal, what are the changes you need to make in your life that will propel you forward toward your dream? There are all sorts of different nuances for different people when it comes to making those positive changes in your life and taking it One Beat at a Time.

For example, maybe your beat change in the next hour is establishing a one-on-one meeting with your boss since e-mail doesn't seem to be getting your messages across to them very well. Set up ten minutes for that change in your mode of communication because you can acknowledge that email and texts may work best for you, but also that they're not for everyone.

Let's say you want to have really effective communication and really connect with your supervisor because you value your job and hope that, down the road, something good might come of it. Once you have that ten-minute face-to-face conversation, you wait for the response. You need to wait and see whether this was a successful, effective beat change or not. If the response comes up positive, then you know that it was effective.

Now, you can continue to trust that beat change and the good decision-making skills you had to go ahead and test out that beat change in the first place.

What we are talking about is a feedback loop. You're always assessing the effectiveness of your beat changes. You're assessing how well they worked and using that information to gain confidence in the choices that you're making.

BREAK DOWN GOALS INTO ACTIONABLE OBJECTIVES

If you are in a position of leadership, you can think of this as breaking it down. Once the big goal is set, break it down into smaller, measurable objectives. These should focus on immediate tasks and outcomes that will directly contribute to the broader goal. This is creating a One Beat at a Time roadmap, which we will describe in the "Create Your Best Role" section of this chapter.

How can you develop ideas for beat changes? Where do they come from? Do we just imagine them and improvise? Or do we sit down and strategize? To begin with, you could brainstorm a list or talk to a friend about it. You can also listen to your intuition, because deep down inside we most always know what it is we need to change in our lives.

If you're an A-type person, you might need a list or a chart to plan this out. But if you're more of a go-with-the-flow type of person, you might just make it up as you go along and try different things until something works. For some people, sometimes it's more about asking hard questions of themselves to find the next steps.

The truth is, all of the above are fair game for choosing and deciding on beat changes that can help you achieve your goals. You can plan or be impromptu, but often, it's just about trusting your intuition.

LISTENING TO YOUR INNER VOICE

When you sharpen your inner voice and allow people you trust in your life to bounce that inner voice's words off of, you amplify your power tremendously. Other ways you can find beat change ideas that will best fit you are through mentors, coaches, therapists, and even doctors, who sometimes have great ideas for small changes you can make in your daily routine to be healthier. Some people can figure things out independently, and others need people around them to support and brainstorm with them.

Dr. Lennie has a poignant story about finding his "why" and choosing his beat changes to become healthier. One day, he was at Disney World, sitting on a bench to rest for a minute, and a woman sat down next to him. She looked to be in her seventies and told him she was there with her grandchildren, but she needed to sit on that bench because she was so tired and her legs were so worn out.

She told him she wished she had the energy to play with her grandchildren. This one moment led Dr. Lennie to set the goal of being healthy enough to walk around and enjoy his grandchildren at Disney World. Sometimes, we see someone like that, and because there's something about them that we know we don't want in our future, it helps us realize what we do want in our future.

Some people need to build their confidence in trying new things. They need to learn to lean into their fears and face them. This type of person shouldn't rush to create a beat change. They need to sit with their reality and get to know their "why" better so they can be authentic to who they are and who they want to be, rather than trying to be someone else. Find the changes that are a good fit for you and align with your desired outcomes in life.

Another thing Dr. Lennie tries to do is to tell Dr. Carmen how much he loves her every day. She often tells him she loves him, since it comes naturally to her, but because of his given circumstances and the fact that in his childhood, no one ever said those words, it doesn't come naturally to him. But that is one of his goals toward building a healthy, loving family relationship. Each time he says it, it is just another small beat, and he has to stretch to remember to do it sometimes, but he is working on it because that is who he wants to be.

Beat changes are about taking things one day at a time to accomplish whatever we need to accomplish. That's the bottom line. So even though we are addressing these small individual beats, we are making these beat changes because the overall driving force is that we're trying to accomplish something much bigger, aligned with our "why." We are trying to get a short-term win that eventually will become a long-term win.

BEAT CHANGES AND AUTHENTICITY

Dr. Carmen has a good friend she's known for years. This friend often says that if she were running our business, she would be on social media daily, doing Facebook Live and those types of posts. We go to these great resorts and get audiences of hundreds of people, and she thinks we should be posting about it online. But that's not who we are—yet.

Dr. Carmen just wants to be in the room with people, know every single person's name, and really have a personal connection with them. She wants to help people feel seen and give them space to explore their pain. That's her social media, her word-spreading strategy. The point is that Dr. Carmen's approach to beat changes is to only make the beat changes that work for her and resonate with her so she can live the type of life she has created. She wants to acknowledge that big room full of people and live in that space while she's in it. If she's going to make a beat change in the world of social media, it will be authentic to who she is.

This doesn't mean she doesn't ever want to use social media. But it does mean that when she does it, it will look very different than what some people might try to impose on her just because it works for them.

Another thing to keep in mind is that you should not be concerned if a beat change you made doesn't work for you. Don't be afraid to throw it out if it doesn't work. Just because it worked for someone else doesn't mean it will work for you, and you have to be mature enough and honest enough to accept what works for you and what doesn't.

It's about self-regulation and self-evaluation. Maybe you'll have to be bold enough to return to a beat that worked last year. Who knows why you stopped doing that, but it doesn't matter; just go back to it. Above all, don't be too hard on yourself if it's not working out. Just because you didn't lose the three pounds this week, keep eating that salad and those smoothies because you know what your overall goal is, and you're taking it One Beat at a Time.

Take a look at what you are doing right now in terms of your goals. If you want a promotion, what are you doing right now that makes you valuable to your workplace? Take a look around and see whether there is someone in your workplace who is not performing at a very high level at a job you'd love to have. How can you step up and perform better to show your supervisors that you can do it better?

GOAL SETTING WITH THE SMARTER FRAMEWORK

The SMARTER framework, a goal-setting methodology, was coined by George T. Doran in 1981 in his paper "There's a S.M.A.R.T. Way to Write Management's Goals and Objectives." Using this framework can help you ask yourself the right questions and get to the best answers that will help you identify your goals and get them set.

The acronym SMARTER stands for:

- Straight and to the point/specific: What do you want to accomplish?
- Metric your meter/measurable: How you'll know if you've achieved your goal
- Attainable/achievable: Whether you have the skills to achieve your goal
- Relatable/relevant: How does your goal relate to your larger objectives?
- Time-bound: By when do you want to achieve your goal?
- Evaluate: How you'll assess your progress
- Refine/readjust: How you'll modify your goal if needed

The SMARTER framework can help you achieve your goals by:

- Defining your objectives
- Setting a completion date
- Improving your ability to reach your goals
- Creating a well-planned, clear, and measurable goal
- Resolving issues with goals that are too broad or vague

You can use the SMARTER framework for both your personal and professional goals—try it out and see for yourself how effective it is to think about goals in terms of these methods and metrics.

Technology comes into play with goal setting as well. Some of us in the older generation aren't quite as handy with tech as younger people are, but you can use apps to track almost any goal you have.

If you're not too handy with tech, you might want to work on that, but don't worry, you can take that One Beat at a Time, too. Look at it as a process.

Take some time here and there to learn new programs and apps. With all of the innovation in our world changing on a daily basis, what are you doing professionally to make a beat change so that you are keeping current? Because if you're not, you might have trouble functioning at your highest level in the long run.

This brings us to another basic principle in our work: Study Your Craft. In acting, it means doing the exercises, learning the methods, keeping up with what others in the field are doing, and other similar learning activities. Studying your craft in life could be about taking a class or buying new software. It could be watching YouTube videos or reading a book.

We all need to step on the AI train and at least understand it and know how to use it if we need to, but it can be overwhelming to wrap our brains around sometimes. Our advice is to take it One Beat at a Time. Make small shifts, learn small chunks of it that align with your motivations, and eventually, you'll get to the level of expertise that is right for you.

When our business fell apart in 2015, we were desperate. We had lost our very large anchor contract, and we kept thinking we had to find another big contract. But we remembered to think in terms of One Beat at a Time, and we started getting smaller contracts, and they started to add up. Then, we could build from there, and the smaller contracts grew.

What's more, we realized that the smaller contracts were actually more valuable because if we lost one, we could replace it more easily, and we wouldn't be decimated like we'd been when we'd lost our one huge contract in early 2015. We followed up this beat change with another: We worked on improving our follow-up with clients and sending notes thanking them for allowing us to serve them.

Another change we made was to make a point of continuing to find ways to indulge in the cultural outings our family had gotten used to. We saved up and got nosebleed seats for that Broadway show. We bought goods at the dollar stores whenever possible, and occasionally, we would still splurge on a nice dinner out. There are other changes we made that will be discussed in later chapters, but that rebuilding period was filled with beat changes, and eventually, they all added up and got us to where we are now.

Using your wants, needs, and must-haves to determine how to prioritize the actions we need to take is essential. If you align your goal setting and plans of action in beat changes with your levels of motivation, your beat changes will reflect that prioritization. You can work on one thing at a time, starting with the most urgent. We can't have it all, and certainly not at the same time. Some goals will take longer than others.

When we work with our clients, we tend to break it up by using and tracing an actual road. One side of the road acts as the personal side, and the other side of the road is for the professional. You can see examples of this at the end of this chapter in the "Create Your Best Role" section.

We have also learned that every beat can be perceived as a Unit of Life. Hence, Alexandra Kamomann gives us this scenario to consider as we start to map out each beat of life, one at a time:

She advises that we analyze the areas of "where to play" and "how to win" in our professional lives. In other words, you need to define your playing field (which industries, geographies, customer segments, and product categories you want to operate within) and what your unique competitive advantage will be (what price, value proposition, supply chain setup, and distribution).

As we are moving along the road, based upon the goals and objectives we have, we will break those down into smaller "beats," to establish our beats, otherwise known as our Units of Life.

This will then allow us to understand how we will transition from one beat to the next. It will also inform us of what we are looking for that will help us to identify when we know that we've accomplished a goal and it's time to move on from one to the next.

Sometimes, we stay stuck working a beat because we really haven't identified what's in it for us or what we're looking for. It's important to get a sense that we've attained a certain amount of what's needed in order to move to the next beat of life.

Beats are significant, even if it's just about taking a pause. This still counts as taking action, and there is a purpose behind that stillness. As you create and outline your roadmap, consider both your micro and macro transitions in life. Visualizing your roadmap can help you identify these beats and transitions, enhance new ideas, and recognize the opportunity to repeat habits that are effective. Clearly mark your beat changes in life while considering a few suggested questions. By all means, feel free to construct your own prompts and go for it.

Here are some guiding questions to ask yourself:

- What are my short-term and long-term goals?
- What do I need in order to pursue these goals?
- Who do I need to know, and how do I get access?
- What might my emotional state be when I accomplish this Beat moment in my life?
- Who will benefit from my beat changes?
- How will I know that the beat change happened (how will I know I conquered the beat change)?
- How will this inform my upcoming goals and motivations in life?

At Dramatic Solutions, we believe it is vital to allow yourself to see that the small things really matter. Small mindset changes, tiny shifts in your choices, and minimal tweaks to your habits can really make all the difference.

Even though we had a very challenging experience at our franchise with Pridestaff, it did underscore the lesson of the beat change that we'd learned years earlier in our acting studies: Positive outcomes are created one call at a time, one day at a time, and One Beat at a Time.

While it's vital to think about beat changes and breaking our forward progress down into small chunks, one of the most critical areas we need to focus on as we pursue our goals based on our "why" is how we choose our supporting cast. Relationships are complicated and sometimes messy, but finding the right people, the "good actors" who will support us on our journey, is essential to playing our best role in life. In the next chapter, we will examine the incremental changes you can make when dealing with Your Dramatic Conflict in life.

CREATE YOUR BEST ROLE

Act Three: One Beat at a Time

Creating and organizing roadmaps is both exciting and informative. Before designing your personal roadmap and professional roadmap, one of the first steps you must do is identify whether you want to break your personal roadmap down into quarters of your life, seasons of your life, or some other chronological framework. For your professional roadmap, you will want to break it up in terms of very specific action goals, and those will be unique to your professional situation.

Ultimately, you will find yourself with two different roadmaps: one for professional planning and goal setting and the other for personal self-evaluation and goal setting.

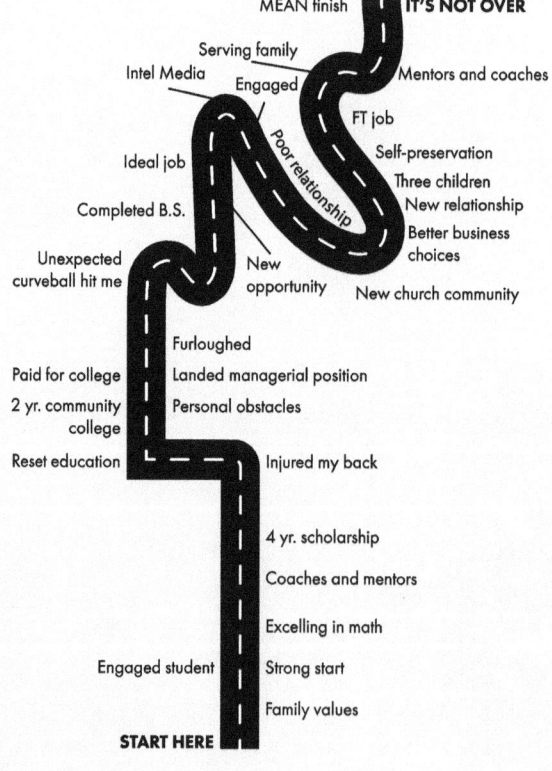

Roadmap Examples

Here are examples of personal and professional roadmaps broken up in quarters.

Reflection:

Once you've completed a roadmap, write a sentence or two answering the following questions.

- How does this roadmap directly align with our overall business objectives and strategy?
- What are the key market trends and customer needs this roadmap is addressing?
- How does this roadmap contribute to achieving our long-term vision?

Prioritization:

- What criteria were used to prioritize the initiatives on this roadmap?
- How were the "must-have" features differentiated from "nice-to-have" features?
- What is the rationale behind the sequencing of initiatives?

Feasibility:

- What are the potential risks and challenges associated with this roadmap?
- What contingency plans are in place to mitigate these risks?
- Have we adequately considered resource availability (people, budget, technology) for each initiative?

Timeline and Milestones:

- Are the deadlines on this roadmap realistic and achievable?
- How are milestones defined and tracked to measure progress?
- What is the process for managing scope changes and potential delays?

Dependencies:

- What are the key dependencies between different initiatives on the roadmap?
- How are we mitigating potential issues arising from these dependencies?
- Are there any external dependencies that could impact the timeline?

Impact and Measurement:

- How will we measure the success of each initiative on the roadmap?
- What key performance indicators (KPIs) will be used to track progress?
- What is the expected return on investment (ROI) for each major initiative?

Communication and Stakeholder Management:

- How will stakeholders be kept informed about the progress of the roadmap?
- What communication channels will be used to share updates and address concerns?
- How will we manage feedback from stakeholders and incorporate it into the roadmap?

ACT FOUR

YOUR DRAMATIC CONFLICT

"Only John can drive somebody that crazy."
—Bonnie Bedelia as Holly in *Die Hard*

When the dean at the university where Dr. Lennie chaired the theater department told him that everything would be fine in 2014, Dr. Lennie believed her. But it wasn't fine at all; Dr. Lennie's position was about to be dissolved, and he, in fact, was about to lose his job there. It was a huge blow, and Dr. Lennie was angry at the deception, the politics, and the decisions. It was not only about himself, but also all the students who believed in the power of theater, who would lose their theater department. It upset him that the university could so easily lose sight of how his students thrived in many careers because of theater. But sadly, the decisions being made by the university weren't about the students' futures; they were about the university's future. During this time, Dr. Lennie thought, felt, and said many unpleasant things.

It was even infuriating for him at times. Instead of saying, "Look, in a year, you're not going to have a job," so he could prepare, his dean said, "We're going to try and work it out. We'll probably make the theater department a minor instead of a major, and then we want to keep you on to run that program." But that wasn't the case; they planned to let him go. In Dr. Lennie's opinion, they knew it all along and were simply not being transparent.

He realizes now that it wasn't personal; the university had its own motivations. They simply weren't planning to continue the program, and these things happen in academia. They knew it would benefit them to string Dr. Lennie along in the fall so he could get his current students closer to graduation in the spring. At the time, though, he was definitely doing what is known as "taking the bait" by letting it upset him so much.

Your Dramatic Conflict is so often rooted in taking the bait. As the saying goes, it's not what happens to you that matters; it's how you react to it. When we react negatively to what we perceive as a negative situation, it creates an even more negative situation.

As it all unfolded in late 2014 and early 2015, Dr. Lennie was in a great deal of distress. He was frustrated and angry. Even now, when he reflects on it, it brings up feelings. It was a tough time for both of us, and it was just one of many events that tempted us to take the bait sometimes and lose our temper, get upset, and possibly make things worse. We had good reason to be upset: We had lost contracts, there were untruths being spread about us around town, and we were caught up in rivalries and betrayals. But we decided we were not going to let this ruin us. We were going to keep our faith, hang on to our love for each other and for our children, and get through it together.

Taking the bait is a sure sign that you have gotten engaged in a negative way with Your Dramatic Conflict. The way to deal with it is to simply catch yourself. Raise your awareness when you feel yourself getting upset. Ask yourself if you are taking the bait.

During our downslide, we took the bait sometimes, but just as often, we were able to catch ourselves and get back on track.

When we tried to sell the house that year, we did so because we had descended into desperation mode. No one was actually baiting us at that time, but financially, we felt that desperation, and that made us start to take the bait and react impulsively. The dramatic conflict was within us as we wrestled with what to do about the house. We spiraled out, thinking, *If we don't sell today, we might not be able to do it tomorrow, so why don't we just get rid of it?* That would have been an easy out, and we were panicked. But fortunately, fate was on our side. The house didn't sell right away, so we had time to realize it was not the right choice to sell it, and we were able to keep it.

IN ACTING

Taking the bait is reacting and almost always overreacting. It's a sure way to become embroiled in Your Dramatic Conflict, and it usually involves other people, especially on the stage, because conflict is a necessary element of drama. Conflict itself is necessary for a story. Without conflict, you have no story. Characters are always taking the bait—that's one of the pleasures of drama. Two opposing forces with opposing motivations must face off against each other for a good story to occur.

The ancient scholar of drama, Aristotle, knew this in 330 BCE. In his book *The Poetics*, he writes, "Conflict is the driving force of drama, particularly in tragedy, where it is presented as a central struggle between opposing forces within the plot, often arising from a protagonist's flawed decisions or tragic flaw, which ultimately leads to their downfall and the audience's experience of catharsis (emotional release) through pity and fear."[5]

The title of our book is *Good Drama!* for a reason. Drama is not necessarily bad! Drama can be used for growth if you avoid taking the bait and instead use the drama as an opportunity to learn and

---

5 Aristotle. *The Poetics of Aristotle*. Accessed August 6, 2025. https://www.amherst.edu/system/files/media/1812/The%252520Poetics%252520of%252520Aristotle%25252C%252520by%252520Aristotle.pdf.

grow. Your Dramatic Conflict can be either a force for good or a destructive force in your life. It depends on how you deal with it.

UNHEALTHY CONFLICT

A playwright writing a play must include a great deal of conflict both between and within the characters. Otherwise, no one would bother coming to see the play. But in real life, we don't want to be in constant heated conflict with others. That's not healthy, and it's definitely not productive in the workplace or at home.

How do you confront conflict? When you're in the heat of the moment, what can you do to keep from being drawn into a disagreement? We recently experienced this while working with an organization in the school system. There were conflicts between teachers, and we worked with them to help them understand that the only thing someone can control is themself.

To explain this, we use the simple prompt "See Me Before He or She." This means checking in with yourself. You're mad at somebody, and there is dramatic conflict, but what is going on with you that you haven't resolved? Are you questioning why you're getting drawn into this conflict? Or are you just letting your emotional reaction run the show?

Consider that this problem might be because of the other person (He or She), or it might be because of you (Me). If you think to yourself, *See Me Before He or She*, you might realize that you are part of the problem. That might be due to you not getting your needs met in some way. The other person might have their own problems for the same reason.

It's important to identify the two different types of Your Dramatic Conflict—internal and external. Ask yourself what internal conflicts you might have with yourself. How do you deal with those problems? If you're able to know yourself well enough to recognize that when you start feeling bad and are exhibiting negative behavior, you could be experiencing inner conflict about something, and you'll have an easier time not taking the bait. Just because the conflict starts as an inner one doesn't mean you won't easily take the bait with someone about it and get into conflict. You can try to catch it before that happens by staying mindful of what's going on inside you.

You might be dealing with someone who has distorted thinking. Maybe they grew up around people who gossiped a lot and now often think others are talking about them when they're not. They have an inner monologue in their head that they have to deal with, making it difficult for them to socialize. They are constantly getting into conflict because of it, but the problem isn't the people around them; it's within them and caused by their limiting beliefs.

In the theater, this inner conflict that creates a lot of unpleasant chatter within a person is called your inner monologue. In real life, it can be a sign of cognitive distortion, which is quite common and can cause a lot of problems. Sometimes, people project their own issues and neuroses onto others. They unwittingly accuse others of doing something that they themselves are doing. There are many types of cognitive distortions, but projection is common and often leads to conflict and a lot of baiting.

Some common cognitive distortions you may be familiar with are:[6]

- Black-and-white (or all-or-nothing) thinking: *I never have anything interesting to say.*
- Jumping to conclusions (or mind reading): *The doctor is going to tell me I have cancer.*
- Personalization: *Our team lost because of me.*
- Should-ing and must-ing (using language that is self-critical that puts a lot of pressure on you): *I should be losing weight.*
- Mental filter (focusing on the negative, such as the one aspect

---

6   Harvard Health Publishing. "How to recognize and tame your cognitive distortions." Harvard Health Blog. Accessed August 6, 2025. https://www.health.harvard.edu/blog/how-to-recognize-and-tame-your-cognitive-distortions-202205042738.

of a health change in which you didn't do well): *I am terrible at getting enough sleep.*
- Overgeneralization: *I'll never find a partner.*
- Magnification and minimization (magnifying the negative, minimizing the positive): *It was just one healthy meal.*
- Fortune-telling: *My cholesterol is going to be sky-high.*
- Comparison (comparing just one part of your performance or situation to another's, which you don't really know, so that it makes you appear in a negative light): *All of my coworkers are happier than I am.*
- Catastrophizing (combination of fortune-telling and all-or-nothing thinking; blowing things out of proportion): *This spot on my skin is probably skin cancer; I'll be dead soon.*
- Labeling: *I'm just not a healthy person.*
- Disqualifying the positive: *I answered that well, but it was a lucky guess.*

Cognitive distortions can be common in various mental health conditions, such as anxiety, depression, and obsessive-compulsive disorder. It's important to be aware of these distortions and challenge them when they occur to promote healthier thinking patterns.

If we see it as an opportunity, we can grow from conflict. We can realize that conflict is necessary in our lives and often healthy. When we are in a disagreement and listen to each other, it's an opportunity to learn from that confrontation. If you're open enough to have that conversation rather than falling into passive or passive-aggressive behavior and can honestly assert yourself in a disagreement in such a way that both you and the other person grow from it, that is healthy.

Unfortunately, many people avoid conflict and think all conflict is bad. But in reality, it can help you see things from someone else's perspective. One of the things we focus on in our trainings is understanding other people's perspectives, especially in terms of how they perceive the world. How do you experience the world?

THE LENS WE SEE OUR WORLD THROUGH

Generally, people fall into one of three categories regarding how they perceive the world: they either perceive it through action, emotion, or thought. In the context of not taking the bait, not understanding how someone else perceives the world is a significant cause of many disagreements. People are swept up in dramatic conflict because they are either baiting other people or taking other people's bait. They're doing this because they are not perceiving the world in the same way as the other person.

Here's the blessing in disguise: If we know that everyone perceives the world primarily through one of these different lenses—and that approximately two-thirds of the world might see things differently than we do because of this—we are much better able to tolerate others and accept each other's differences. If you first acknowledge and accept that other people view the world differently from you and if you can recognize that you, too, have your own lens through which you interpret what is happening around you, so much miscommunication can be avoided.

Maybe your boss is having a strange reaction—ignoring you or not reading your emails. Maybe this is not because you did something wrong but because she views the world through an emotional lens and she is dealing with her own emotions, not yours. When you realize this, you can have compassion for her instead of being irritated that she is upset and possibly making the situation worse.

Emotional perceivers can have a little more trouble with not taking the bait because they can get caught up in the feelings of a situation, whereas action-oriented perceivers just decide on a course of action and, in a way, can let it go. Neither is better than the other.

Dr. Lennie perceives the world through thoughts and beliefs, so he reasons to himself that he can just think it through and honor his ideas about something with someone if it's an employee. He may decide it would be best to let that person go. He focuses on taking action and moving forward. He thinks, *Soon, this person will no longer be here. I'm not going to get into it with him or worry about it because it is what it is.*

He used to get upset and try to change them, but it never worked out because their personality just didn't match his, so why bother? You can't change other people. You want people to see things the way you see them. But you can't control others; you can't change them either. You may support them and make edits and help them reset and repair, but only if the person is motivated to do so and open to the growth.

EUSTRESS

There are two different types of stress, and one is actually good for you. Eustress, as opposed to stress, can make us a little uncomfortable for positive reasons and can help us with challenges that are exciting and healthy for us. If you have to run a race or give a speech, you will feel the adrenaline running through your body and other chemicals reacting in anticipation of the event. Your body is responding to something positive so that you can use those chemicals and that energy for your success. Eustress (positive stress) can help you, especially if you use your breath to channel the excess energy in a positive way. There are times when being around somebody makes us nervous or unsettled, and we can use that information to calm ourselves down or find our inner strength in some way.

According to Hans Selye, a renowned Canadian authority on stress, stress itself is neither inherently good nor bad—stress is an opportunity.[7] Without stress, there is no life. Whether stress is beneficial or harmful depends on how individuals respond to it. The same activity can be experienced as eustress for some and distress for others.

For example, imagine being asked right this minute to stand and speak in front of five hundred people about Hans Selye's model of

---

[7] Lumen Learning. "What Is Stress?" *Introduction to Psychology.* Accessed August 6, 2025. https://courses.lumenlearning.com/suny-intropsychmaster/chapter/what-is-stress/.

stress. Some of you might feel uncomfortable and say, "That's not fair! I need time to rehearse. I'm not ready to do that. I don't know the material well enough."

For those of us who feel this way, it would be distressful. On the other hand, some of us might think, *Yeah, I can do that! I'll show them how it should be explained.* For those who respond this way, it would be eustressful. Eustress, in this context, is simply the result of being asked to use muscles (whether literal or figurative) that are not yet well developed.

I'M OK; YOU'RE OK

I'm OK–You're OK is the title of a 1967 bestselling self-help book by psychiatrist Thomas A. Harris, MD. We have adopted his title and parts of his theory to advocate using the phrase "I'm OK; you're OK" as a method of handling Your Dramatic Conflict. We do this because we see that a pervasive source of conflict between people is their lack of an "I'm OK; you're OK" attitude. Instead, they either have an "I'm OK; you're not OK" attitude or an "I'm not OK; you're OK" viewpoint. This simple concept can act as a transformative instructor, helping you to not take the bait and resolve Your Dramatic Conflict in many situations.

Just because "I'm OK and you're OK," it doesn't mean we aren't different. For instance, when someone around Dr. Carmen neglects to say thank you or isn't kind, it bothers her. But they're not necessarily bad people. They might not have been taught to say thank you. Don't take it personally. Not taking things personally is a tremendously helpful strategy for not taking the bait.

The point is to remember not just that I'm OK and you're OK, but also to remember that we are all OK.

AWARENESS

What are some strategies for becoming aware of when you're about to take the bait or when you don't need to take the bait? How do you know what kind of thoughts or questions you should be asking? What signs should you be looking for?

One strategy is tone matching. If you miss a deadline and your supervisor asks in a sharp tone, "Why are you turning in this report late?," be aware of whether you're accidentally matching their tone, escalating the conflict. If they seem heated, you can choose to stay calm. If someone's taking you down a rabbit hole of disagreement, and voices are starting to get loud or heated, can you reset your own tone? Trying to avoid tone matching can help you rise above a situation so you don't take the bait.

If you feel discomfort in your body, it can help you become aware that you're starting to take the bait. Physical tension starts to build. Your breath, in particular, can change; it might not be as relaxed or centered. You start to lose your feelings of control and focus. The patterns of the breath aren't as calm and predictable. You might even feel your breath getting away from you—moving from a control breath state to a more vulnerable and less controlled state, even getting to the point where there's a shortness of breath. It might even shift to your chest, your neck, or your nose. Some people even start to breathe up in their foreheads when they're stressed, as difficult as it is to believe. The point is that awareness of your breath and how it's changing can help you notice when you might be taking the bait.

If you miss those signs that you're taking the bait, you might need someone else to tell you, "Hey, you know what? They're baiting you. You might not want to take the bait." Having good actors around you helps with this strategy to transform Your Dramatic Conflict into an opportunity for growth.

From Dr. Carmen's perspective, Dr. Lennie is not just a good actor; he's a great actor. She thinks he should get an award for being the "King of Baiting Radar." He's the one who will most often say,

"Dr. Carmen, you're taking the bait. Don't take the bait." And lately, she's been getting better about not taking the bait.

When Dr. Lennie's father died about a year and a half before we started writing this book, he would get frustrated about things a little more quickly. If he snapped or said something to Dr. Carmen, she kept in mind that distress can cause someone to take the bait much more automatically. She tried to acknowledge his distress and think to herself, *He's not mad at me. He's just going through something.* That way, there was no argument. This is a perfect example of not taking the bait on Dr. Carmen's part.

Recently, Dr. Carmen got into a dispute with a bureaucrat she had to deal with for our business. She felt this person was attacking her. She was having thoughts like, *You're a government worker. Where's your customer service training? Where's your professionalism?* It was a very difficult situation. Dr. Carmen doesn't like conflict. She loves being a peacemaker. So this really got to her.

Dr. Carmen had multiple conversations with the person, and when the woman sent her an encrypted email response, it was the straw that finally broke the camel's back. By this point in time, Dr. Carmen was livid. She didn't respond to the email because it was encrypted, and it would take a lot of time and energy for her to even open the message.

So she picked up the phone and called this woman. She said something like, "Why are you sending this email when I'm doing exactly what you asked?"

Because she was heated, she was taking the bait. She was frustrated and in distress—not tear-your-heart-out distress, but fairly serious distress because she had multiple people whose paperwork she was responsible for pushing through. She was trying to ensure the government did what it was supposed to do and, in essence, was just doing her job. She was motivated by her desire to keep Dramatic Solutions moving forward.

They were on the phone for an intense fifteen minutes of dramatic conflict. They were just talking over each other and at each other.

Finally, Dr. Carmen became aware of what was going on within her. She muted her phone, looked at Dr. Lennie, and said, "I don't like this person." We knew at that moment that it had become personal; Dr. Carmen was taking the bait! Her talent was not even going to be available to her because she was so mad.

She took a deep breath and muttered, "This is a lot." Then, she unmuted her phone and said, much more calmly, "You know, these are people's livelihoods. They need to pay their bills. They want to put basic food on the table for their families, and they want to continue to be supportive leaders in this high-needs community. I'm just asking you to do whatever you possibly can to make that happen."

EMPATHIZE INSTEAD

The woman on the other end started to listen to her. Maybe she could hear the shift in Dr. Carmen's tone, because she started asking other questions. The woman asked, "Well, what other government agencies do you work with? Do you work with this one? Or that one?" Dr. Carmen said no, and no again. She started getting a little snippy again because the woman kept asking her if she worked with this organization or that organization, and all Dr. Carmen could say was, "No." And then she realized what she should say.

"We don't work with those organizations. But we are working with this one."

The woman replied, "Oh, well, they should have put that down on the paperwork! Maybe I can make something happen."

This phone conversation, which was really bad at first, ended up being a very nice one by the very end. Because Dr. Carmen started trying to empathize with her and add a level of humanizing the situation, her opposition softened.

Another thing Dr. Carmen did well with the government employee was to just stay on the phone. She was still trying to get through to her. It's important that we not give up, not hang up, not throw up our hands and walk away. Why? Because ultimately, that is not going to lead you to a solution. And what we are talking about here are solutions—Dramatic Solutions.

In the end, Dr. Carmen was able to find her inner calm. She admits it was hard. But she had Dr. Lennie on the side, reminding her, "Don't take the bait, Dr. Carmen. Don't take the bait." Thank goodness for her supporting cast on that day.

This was all in the context of someone we barely knew and don't often have to deal with, but what we got out of that really demonstrates that not taking the bait doesn't happen instantly. Sometimes, even as Dramatic Solutions leaders—supposed masters of this teaching—we're still human beings. It happens to all of us, and it takes time to catch ourselves.

Our society seems designed these days to encourage people to take the bait. There is so much conflict out there right now. Our breathing is off; our body language is off. Sometimes, even our mindset is off, and we are easily triggered. We just have to come back to our humanity so we can find our way and navigate life's natural conflicts a little more peacefully.

It's so easy to jump in and take the bait, and you just have to pull back. Not taking the bait in written communication in a professional setting is just as important as not taking the bait in verbal communication. Take twenty-four hours to respond to a text or an email that is contentious or could be construed as contentious. Dr. Lennie often says, "Don't respond to the text; don't respond to the email now. They don't know if you received it or looked at it yet. Don't respond."

When you have someone who has something you want, it's not going to do you any good to curse them out. Instead, seek to understand rather than to be understood. Try to figure out where they are coming from and what their motivations are, and allow that to help you get to your yes.

Many professional associates and friends of ours are going through similar circumstances related to working and maintaining a drama-free household. Many are also living in a "sandwich generation" scenario with a father, mother, grandparent, or other close relative.

Suddenly, they find themselves being caregivers for both their ancestors and their offspring. Many of our clients are dealing with these kinds of circumstances as well. Sometimes, it helps to remember that as bad as your situation might be, someone else's is probably worse.

Taking the bait can cause a chain reaction in larger organizations, if left unchecked. When a leader in an organization gets upset with the hierarchy above them, they carry those emotions down to the people they manage. The next thing you know, you have a dysfunctional environment and culture in the organization because you're in distress. You're not taking care of yourself, and you're creating a hostile environment.

Keep your eyes on the prize. You do this by staying focused on your motivation and your overall intention. Your overall "why" is the piece that should drive you to ensure you're staying focused on what actually matters, and that can help you to stop taking the bait. In the case of Dr. Carmen and the government official, what really mattered was helping people put food on the table for their kids.

If you are triggered by certain things because of things that happened in your childhood, you're going to battle reactivity and bait-taking for the rest of your life. It will get easier and easier, maybe, as you get better at it. But because of Your Given Circumstances, sometimes you'll get triggered by things.

If you get upset not by something someone does but by how it triggers you, then that's taking the bait when it's not really even their fault. That's overreacting.

Some of what we have to do is look at why we are overreacting. You can ask yourself, *Why am I not handling this well? Why is this bothering me so much? Does it have to do with something that happened to me in childhood or something that I'm still working on?* In the end, this, like everything else, might come back to our given circumstances.

Our kids have definitely helped us learn not to take the bait over the years. For instance, we used to travel every year to Florida, but we don't fly to other places much. We've been content to just drive down to Florida every Christmas and drive to Williamsburg during Thanksgiving.

Meanwhile, when she was a teenager, our daughter's friends were flying to Paris and other places all over the world with their families. One day, she said to us, brokenhearted, "We never do anything. We never go anywhere."

When he heard that, Dr. Lennie had an emotional reaction; he felt upset and unappreciated. Instead of getting into a conflict with her, though, he took some deep breaths; he inhaled and exhaled deeply several times and found his calm. His rational mind could then remind him that our daughter's friends probably look at her and say, "Wow, you get to go to Florida every Christmas!" He knew that we were giving her and her brother priceless family traditions in the way we approached travel.

Dr. Lennie could have said, "What are you talking about? You're so ungrateful! We don't want to go to Paris. We don't travel like that."

Instead, he said, "You can always go to those places. Just save your money and go. If we take you everywhere, you won't be able to enjoy your own adventures when you're an adult."

Because we are both sensitive people who care deeply about other people, we both struggle with taking the bait and sometimes have to really wrestle with it. But because we have developed the work that we have, when we find ourselves getting upset, we do the work. We are able to sit back and realize we're taking the bait and catch ourselves. We tell ourselves, "I'm about to take the bait, but I'm not going there."

THE FOUR STAGES OF LIGHTING

In our work, we use the concept of the spotlight, just like the ones we see on the stage, to illustrate four ways we tend to interact with others (or not) and how we stay in a positive mindset. Thinking about the way you relate to others can help you become more mindful and objective about any conflicts or negative feelings you might have in a personal or professional relationship.

- Dimming Your Light—This stage involves avoiding your own light while giving the spotlight to others. The mindset here is, "You are OK, and I am not OK."
- Spotlighting—In this stage, you are in the spotlight, believing that "I am OK, and you are not OK."
- Blind Spotting—Here, you are avoiding the light altogether, leading to the belief that "I am not OK, and you are not OK."
- Standing in Your Light—This stage occurs when you are aware of your own light and how to move forward with it. The understanding here is, "I am OK, and you are OK."

Here are the emotional outcomes of each stage:

- Dimming Your Light (lose–win)—This stage often results in feelings of victimization, resentment, and a loss of control.
- Spotlighting (win–lose)—This mindset can lead to violating the feelings of others by suggesting that your feelings are more important.
- Blind Spotting (lose–lose)—This stage results in feelings of anger toward yourself and a lack of respect for the feelings of others.
- Standing in Your Light (win–win)—In this stage, you stand up for your beliefs while respecting others' beliefs, leading to a positive and respectful outcome.

The goal is to create win–win situations and stand in your light. When people fail to manage their light, they become vulnerable to taking the bait, leading to internal conflict or conflict with others, often resulting in miscommunication. Miscommunication occurs when a message is not accurately received or understood as intended. It can lead to confusion, misunderstandings, and even conflicts. This miscommunication can happen through verbal, nonverbal, or written channels, influenced by various factors.

When people are standing in their light, they experience many positives in their lives. Their mindset is "I'm OK; you're OK."

However, when individuals enter a state of distress, the positives are replaced with negatives. When people are offstage, their mindset shifts to either "I'm OK; you're not OK" or "I'm not OK; you're OK."

In the movie *Die Hard*, John McClane's estranged wife, Holly, is kidnapped with colleagues by the blackmailing kidnapper Hans Gruber, who storms away from them in fury and smashes a barrel with his rifle. She sees Hans throw this fit and realizes her husband, John McClane, is still alive. She says, "Only John can drive someone that crazy," knowing that Hans's fury could only be ignited by the man she loves. Hans has taken the bait and let John drive him crazy. It's an ironic example of how certain people, usually those who've created obstacles to our goals, can make us lose our cool completely.

Who are you letting drive you crazy? Who will win?

Conflict is always going to arise in life. Take stock of how you deal with it in your life and see how you can grow from it rather than let it cause unhealthy stress in your life.

When you find yourself falling into conflict, don't let people draw you into disagreement and ignite your freeze, fawn, fight-or-flight instincts. Instead, stop and examine what those opposing forces are. See their side so that you can grow. Remember that you can avoid taking the bait by stepping back and analyzing this problem like a dramatist would. What is the conflict? What are the opposing forces? What is your motivation in this situation? What is theirs? How can you use this situation as an opportunity for growth?

EMOTIONAL INTELLIGENCE

Emotional intelligence (EI), also referred to as emotional quotient (EQ), is the ability to recognize, understand, manage, and influence your own emotions, as well as the emotions of others. It involves a combination of self-awareness, self-regulation, motivation, empathy, and social skills.

People with high emotional intelligence tend to have better mental health, job performance, and leadership skills because they can navigate interpersonal relationships more effectively.

Here are the five key components of emotional intelligence:

- Self-awareness
- Self-regulation
- Motivation
- Empathy
- Social skills

Many everyday situations require us to demonstrate strong social-emotional skills to get along with others in life. These include positive situations such as sharing and collaboration, building healthy relationships, and completing tasks. They are also needed to cope with some negative situations, such as handling a bully, dealing with someone who is cheating in some way, or coping with traumatic situations such as death and divorce.

It's important to improve your emotional intelligence for so many reasons: your career, your relationships, your physical and mental health, and many more.

Here are a few examples of how to improve your emotional intelligence:

- Practice mindfulness—Mindfulness and meditation help us create some distance between our deeper selves and all of the mental and emotional activity we experience inside ourselves. Our "inner monologues" like to go on and on, and sometimes, we can find ourselves getting upset simply because we are thinking too much! Take time throughout each day to get quiet and focus on your breath or the sensations in your body and around you. Be in the moment and allow all those thoughts and feelings to pass over you like clouds in the sky.

- Seek feedback—It's important and often very useful to ask others for clarification if you're confused or reassurance if you're concerned about how something is turning out.
- Reflect on your experiences—Take time to journal or just quietly reflect on your experiences, especially if they are upsetting you in some way.
- Develop empathy—Empathy is a tremendous strength that can help you see the other person's perspective if you are in a conflict.
- Learn to manage stress—Exercise, breathwork, healthy communication, and plenty of rest are just a few strategies for managing stress.

Emotional intelligence is a skill that can be developed and strengthened over time with practice and intentional effort. By improving your EI, you can build better relationships, manage stress more effectively, and improve your overall well-being.

Learning to refrain from taking the bait doesn't happen overnight; it's one of those "beat changes" we all need to make. Staying aware of when you might be on the verge of engaging in conflict helps you resist that temptation.

Conflict is a natural occurrence in human relationships, and it is ongoing work. Over and over, you have to think about who the characters in your drama are and whether they are positive additions to your life.

When our business tanked, we didn't jump back up and start to rebuild it from scratch right away. For a while, Dr. Lennie was still trying to make teaching his focus, and Dr. Carmen was working on other business options, such as the franchise opportunity. But at a certain point, we just knew we had to get back on track and keep pursuing our entrepreneurial dream.

In retrospect, losing his job at the university was the best thing that ever happened to Dr. Lennie. It was the very definition of Good Drama. If Dr. Lennie had stayed working for the university, we wouldn't be doing the amazing work we are doing now. We wouldn't be writing this book. We also wouldn't have become as successful financially.

We were in the midst of our dramatic conflict, but we weren't going to take the bait; we just had to make some big changes to how we were doing things. What we learned from that is the next Dramatic Solutions principle: Setting the Stage for your success. Once you have a clear vision of yourself playing your best role, it's time to create the environment and the mindset to truly become it.

CREATE YOUR BEST ROLE

Act Four: Your Dramatic Conflict

The Four Stages of Lighting helps you think about how you can be more effective in your relationships by staying mindful of any conflicts or negative feelings you might have.

Here are the emotional outcomes of each stage:

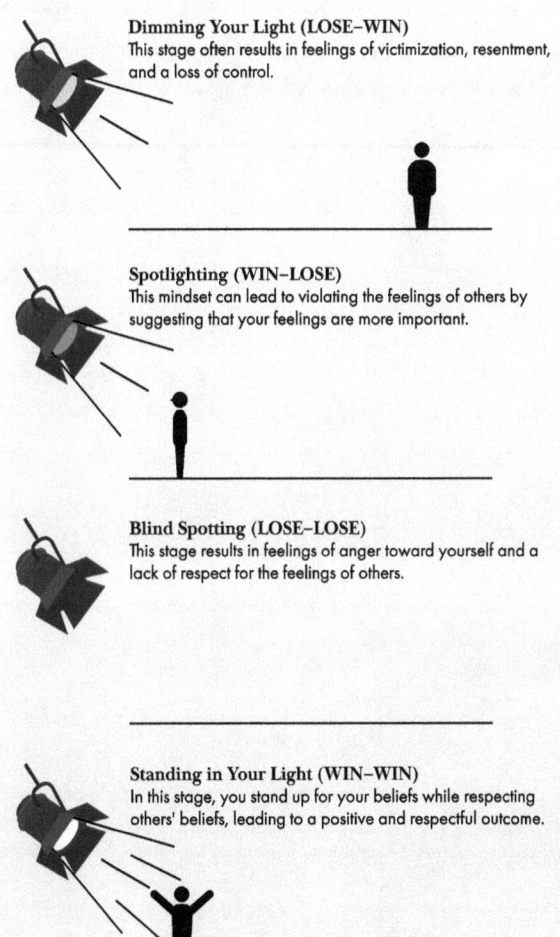

Dimming Your Light (LOSE–WIN)
This stage often results in feelings of victimization, resentment, and a loss of control.

Spotlighting (WIN–LOSE)
This mindset can lead to violating the feelings of others by suggesting that your feelings are more important.

Blind Spotting (LOSE–LOSE)
This stage results in feelings of anger toward yourself and a lack of respect for the feelings of others.

Standing in Your Light (WIN–WIN)
In this stage, you stand up for your beliefs while respecting others' beliefs, leading to a positive and respectful outcome.

Activity:

Make a list of three to five situations you've been in when you were Dimming Your Light.

Then do the same for the other three stages.

Reflection:

Write about or discuss with someone close to you how you could have done things differently in one of the times you weren't Standing in Your Light and experiencing the win–win balance in a relationship?

ACT FIVE

YOUR SUPPORTING CAST

"You make me want to be a better man."
—Jack Nicholson as Melvin in *As Good as It Gets*

We are both originally from Washington, DC, but we never knew each other growing up. Dr. Lennie grew up in a rough part of town—Southeast Washington, DC—and attended public school there. Dr. Carmen grew up in the more middle-class DC/Maryland area and started out in public school but attended Catholic school for junior high and high school.

As we shared earlier, we met in New York City while we were both studying acting at the American Musical and Dramatic Academy. If we had met in DC, we are fairly sure we would never have connected. When we met, Dr. Lennie had a perception, a stereotype really, about girls who grew up in Maryland and were in Catholic school. Dr. Carmen had a perception of guys who grew up in Southeast DC as guys who make bad choices. Dr. Carmen even had friends and mentors who told her to stay away from Dr. Lennie because of where he was from and where he grew up. Colorism came into play when some of Dr. Carmen's friends thought she shouldn't date Dr. Lennie just because he was a darker black person than she was.

Dr. Carmen could have been blinded by stereotyping and never seen how much he loved his mother. Early on in our relationship, Dr. Lennie's mom became ill. Dr. Carmen remembers the commitment he showed by going to the hospital all the time and visiting her. She saw that when his mom would call, he would jump for her. Because of Dr. Carmen's upbringing, seeing a man show that kind of affection for his mom made an impression on her. She was raised to believe that if a man treats his mother well, it's likely that he will do the same for you.

We met at a party when someone introduced us, saying, "Hey, you're both from DC." We started chatting, and Dr. Lennie shared his desire to work with young people. By this time, he had already become interested in giving back to the community through acting. And Dr. Carmen was interested in the same thing. So we started out as friends and worked together for a theater company based in New York City. We really connected, most likely because we had that same dream. At a certain point, we realized we had each other's backs and were supporting each other on our journeys.

Our relationship came out of that—we started out as friends, partners, a support system. As pretty as Dr. Carmen is ("gorgeous," as Dr. Lennie puts it), Dr. Lennie wasn't looking at that alone. He saw her as a good friend. In fact, he was trying to fix her up with a friend of his. But she wasn't having any of it. To this day, Dr. Carmen doesn't know what Dr. Lennie was thinking, fixing her up with his friend Glenn. He claims he only saw her as a good person and a good friend, and he honestly wanted her to be with a good guy. He could see that she was an exceptionally good person, and she could see the same about him, too.

The love and support grew until we were "acting as if" we were in a relationship, even though we weren't.

Dr. Lennie found himself engaging in relationship behaviors without even realizing it. When Dr. Carmen would mention, "I'm going to get my hair done," he would ask, "Where are you going?" and she would respond, "I'm going to Brooklyn." Then Dr. Lennie would insist, "Oh, I'm going with you." Even if she was going somewhere late at night, he would go with her and wait, driven by his desire to ensure her safety.

We both remember the day Cupid struck—the moment that changed everything. We were driving back to New York City from the DC area, where we had been working on a project together. We decided to create a talk show to help Dr. Carmen in her pursuit of becoming the Oprah Winfrey of the time, collaborating with a couple of actor friends from New York City. As we all drove back, we decided that since Dr. Lennie lived in Harlem and Dr. Carmen lived in Brooklyn, we would drop Dr. Carmen off first.

Their mutual friend was driving, and Dr. Lennie was in the front seat next to him. Dr. Carmen was in the back seat when, out of nowhere, Dr. Lennie's hand brushed Dr. Carmen's face. We looked at each other, and both of us felt a rush of emotions. It was a Cupid moment, and it hit us hard.

The whole night, Dr. Lennie felt a mix of excitement and confusion, thinking, *What just happened?* Later that night, when the phone rang, he thought, *Oh my God, she's calling me.* He answered, "Hey, hey, what's up?"

Dr. Carmen simply said, "Hey, what are you doing? I'm coming over." Dr. Lennie felt a wave of anxiety wash over him and, full of nerves, he thought to himself, *Oh Lord.*

Dr. Carmen was always very particular about whom she said yes to or felt attracted to. She wasn't extremely aware of her values at the time, but she had a strong conviction in her faith in Jesus Christ. She had very high standards around what she wanted.

In hindsight, having that knowledge and understanding of how values can dictate our relationships, there were obviously similar values we both shared. One, in particular, was the need and desire to give back to our community, particularly to young people.

Moments of vulnerability, like when we use drive from New York City back to Washington, DC, helped us grow closer to each other, and this is an excellent example of how we can find our supporting cast. We both already knew what we wanted. We had our values already in place, and we knew what we were looking for in a partner.

We connected because we value the humanness of people's needs, and we both wanted to give back. Public service and community service were important to us. And they still are. To this day, we still work in the juvenile corrections space and other areas of government and education.

It's sometimes difficult for people to just be themselves and develop friendships and see if something more happens as a result. But if something does happen out of that, then you may have just found your soulmate.

IN ACTING

In drama, characters are almost always in a relationship with each other. A strong protagonist and antagonist are essential to a great story. If you are the protagonist in your own story, who are the antagonists?

When we talk about building our supporting cast, we are really talking about selectivity. There is extreme selectivity in the casting phase of a play, film, or TV show. Once everyone is cast, the director must decide their physical proximity to each other based on the story. If they're lovers, they're close. If they're enemies, they are running or hiding from each other in some way or possibly even trying to kill each other.

In the process of blocking out the movements of the actors on a stage or a film set, decisions are made about how close two characters will be to each other physically, and these decisions are made on the level of conflict or attraction between them and their needs and motivations. All the roles are valuable; they're all necessary for the story to be entertaining, but that doesn't mean they all have to be close to each other. Someone can be OK, and they can be valuable, but you might prefer that they are valuable from a distance…sometimes even way over there!

In life, often, this is less intentional. People don't always know their values or what they want in their friends, business associates, and romantic partners, so they don't block it out on the stage of their lives and decide who they want close to them and who should be far away. This can lead to a lot of challenges. Do you know what your values and motivations are and what you are looking for in Your Supporting Cast?

Stereotypes can move you forward, but they can also keep you stuck. If we had only been looking at each other's demographics, we probably would not have even taken a second look at each other. We would never have found our soulmates and life partners in each other. Stereotypes can limit people from connecting and act as a stumbling block to building Your Supporting Cast.

Be mindful that your idea of a strong supporting role might come from a typecast. Are you being discriminating, as in selective, in a healthy way? Or are you discriminating against someone because of a stereotype?

GOOD AND BAD ACTORS

At some point in your story, you get to move from what was handed to you in your deck of cards to how you want to play them and with whom. Who do you want to be at the table with you when you play your cards?

Let's face it: There are "good actors" and "bad actors" in this world, and in our lives, we need to be selective about who we hang out with. We are all casting agents as we go through life, and if we want Good Drama in our lives instead of bad drama, we should be looking for people whose values and motivations match our own.

An example of a bad actor would be a manager who makes everybody around them miserable or who really doesn't know their job well. They have the opportunity to lead others and to grow those around them, but instead, they tend to be the distractor that keeps others from doing their work.

A bad actor is often someone who lacks self-esteem, is not secure, and really doesn't have any self-efficacy. They're not really that great at the job; maybe they've been promoted for some other reason. This type of bad actor probably suffers from impostor syndrome. They have the title of manager, and they're hung up on the title, but they don't exemplify any of the characteristics of what it means not just to be a manager but to be a good one. They don't know how to move people. So, they're considered to be, in many of our clients' lives, a bad actor when it comes to management.

Here's another way of thinking about this: Who are the characters you will move forward with, and who are the people you don't want to be around?

When we were working with the staffing franchise, we had a brick-and-mortar location in Prince George's County, Maryland, for almost three years. During those three years, we discovered that when we interfaced with business owners, managers, and project managers who were looking to hire, they were really clear about their criteria. They were very clear about the list of roles and responsibilities of the candidates we should be looking for.

Think about the qualities of those who will be working with you, loving you, or being in your life in some way. Assess their abilities, strengths, and weaknesses, as well as their unique gifts.

Some questions to ask are:

- Am I willing to cast people in my life who challenge me and will play devil's advocate?
- Am I willing to bring people into my life who are maybe doing better than I am and who I can look up to as a model for growth?
- Does the relationship allow you to stay mindful of your boundaries?
- We all need cheerleaders in our lives. Who are my cheerleaders?

This is true in the professional world as well as the personal. When you're choosing employees, business associates, trusted colleagues, and mentors, you might want to ask yourself questions about their character, their goals, and other internal factors. You also might simply want to look at how well they align with your mission and your company's mission.

Whether choosing our supporting cast in business or deciding what kind of people we want in our lives, we need to consider values and traits like loyalty and family devotion, honesty and kindness.

Are there toxic people in your life who are always complaining about others? What can you do about it? Sometimes, it's important to be bold enough to fire people from your company or separate from them in your personal life. It really comes down to your mission and values in life. Does this person align with and support those things? If not, it's time to create some distance.

AVATARS AS TOOLS

How do we want to identify ourselves? Who do we want to be? What type of person do we want around us? The work of envisioning ourselves playing our best role has to be done to inform the choices of our supporting cast. Only then will we be ready to attract like-minded people who can support us to the greatest extent.

Creating our own avatar and the avatars of those closest to us in our lives can help. When you are writing out the description of your avatar for a friend or business associate, think about all of the qualities you appreciate in others. Responsibility, ambition, civility, and wanting to give back are some of ours. What are yours?

Many people miscast their supporting roles. They do this by committing to someone because they are focusing on things that aren't values-driven. As a result, they might miss the person who is a perfect fit for them in terms of their values and morality, not necessarily their looks or bank account. In our opinion, these people are looking for all the wrong things.

For instance, you could be looking for wealth as a criterion for a potential partner or friend, when instead, you could be looking for ambition as a character trait in the people you want around you. We often look for people with attributes that are "shiny." In doing so, we might miss seeing the truly beautiful person who was auditioning for the role and has been in front of us the whole time.

From a professional side, when people are looking at their supporting cast—like hiring managers or HR departments—during their selection and onboarding process, they sometimes miss the person who would be the best supporting cast member. They might overlook someone because they are searching for an Ivy League graduate, not realizing that a candidate from an HBCU (historically Black colleges and universities) actually has the skill set, temperament, and personality needed for the team.

The online content we are all constantly consuming is also a problem. Too often, we get caught up in social media drama and how many thousands of likes we might have. That is superficial appreciation; it's not real. When times get hard, we probably won't see those people who are on our social media feeds as much. People don't generally expose aspects of themselves as much on social media in their most vulnerable moments, so it's important to distinguish between real friends and superficial ones.

WHAT YOU BRING TO THE TABLE

One of the things we run into quite a lot is people who are not in relationships but want to be in one. They have their standards, but those standards can be ridiculous, or they might not even be living up to those standards themselves. We look at them and think, *You want something that looks perfect, but you're not extremely perfect yourself.*

These people have a lot of requirements for a potential mate: They have to make a certain amount of money. They can't have a lot of debt. They have to have a certain level of education. They have to have a nice car and maybe even own real estate. Many people have that kind of measuring stick, often without a lot of awareness of what they themselves would actually bring to the table.

Society supports this attitude. You hear conversations about, "Well, I won't marry for love necessarily. I want someone to be rich, and I won't settle for anything less." And then you see people who take that route and are miserable. They have all these material things, but they put up with too many negatives and are unhappy.

TV shows support this, too. *The Bachelor* shows us how to catch millionaires, and so that's who we think we should be lucky enough to marry. This same dynamic happens in the workplace, too. There's the academic measuring stick we discussed above, but sometimes there are even more subtle things that are more superficial and materialistic than substantial. Do they belong to the right country club or look a certain way physically? Deep down, we all know that those things are not what matters when it comes to how well someone will perform their work.

People are very rarely perfect, and there is always room for growth. The key is to look for potential and progress, not perfection. We see people all the time who aren't willing to go through the journey of growth with anyone. They want their partner or their new employee to be perfect and already have all the success, all the answers, and all the wisdom.

Once we were back to the grind of rebounding in our own business, we had to get clear on what kinds of people were in the world we wanted to be in. We know they were the ones we needed to get solidly back in touch with. We are always working to feel more comfortable and more worthy of being with people who know more than we do.

We learned to value surrounding ourselves with people who are where we want to be, not necessarily where we are. Bringing people around you who support you in every aspect is crucial.

As Dr. Lennie says, we can't keep being in spaces where we're the smartest people in the room. This brings us to the topic of mentors, both in our lives and outside of them.

SETTING YOUR TABLE FOR SUCCESS

In the journey toward personal and professional success, the metaphor of preparing a table becomes a powerful tool for reflection and action. This lesson, drawn from the concept of "Moment Mondays," emphasizes the importance of intentionality in the relationships and environments we cultivate around us. By focusing on key elements—time, abilities, boundaries, list, and engagement—you can create a robust support system that fosters growth and accountability.

THE T IN TABLE: TIME

Time is the foundation of every successful endeavor. It is essential to recognize the significance of inviting the right people into your life during the appropriate season. Being intentional about who you surround yourself with can greatly influence your success. Evaluate your current season and consider who can genuinely contribute to your journey. These individuals will not only provide support but will also hold you accountable, enhancing your capacity for creating wins in your life.

THE A IN TABLE: ABILITIES

Once you have established your team, it's crucial to assess both your abilities and those of the people around you. Self-awareness is key; understand your strengths and areas for improvement, as well as the capabilities of others. This mutual understanding fosters a collaborative environment where everyone can thrive, leading to progressive success. Taking the time to identify and appreciate the diverse abilities present at your table will enable you to leverage these strengths effectively.

THE B IN TABLE: BOUNDARIES

Setting clear boundaries is vital for maintaining the integrity of your table. Understanding your personal and professional limits allows you to engage in healthy and productive relationships. As you define your nonnegotiables, reflect on how far you are willing to stretch them and the potential impact of those choices. Remember, this is your table, and you hold the power to decide who joins you. Cultivating a space that respects your boundaries will empower your interactions and promote mutual respect.

THE L IN TABLE: LIST

Creating a comprehensive list of potential table members is an essential component of your success. Start by identifying your "why"—why do you want each person at your table? Understanding the value they bring to your life will help you select individuals who amplify your mission and support your growth. Keep this list dynamic, remaining open to including new voices that can provide diverse perspectives and constructive criticism. The richness of opinions can enhance discussions and lead to greater insights, ensuring that your table remains a fertile ground for growth and accountability.

THE E IN TABLE: ENGAGEMENT

Finally, it is time to engage. With your table set, it's crucial to embrace the people who have gathered and the resources that will be shared. This is the moment to nourish relationships, exchange ideas, and foster a supportive environment where everyone can learn and grow. Remember, your success is linked to the energy you invest in these connections. Celebrate each moment and the shared journey toward success.

As you prepare your table for success, each element offers a distinct opportunity for reflection and action. By making thoughtful decisions about time, recognizing abilities, establishing boundaries, creating a purposeful list, and engaging fully, you lay the groundwork for a supportive and empowering environment. Your table is a reflection of your commitment to growth and achievement—design it wisely, and enjoy the feast of opportunities it will bring.

VICARIOUS SUPPORT AND MENTORS

We often talk about living vicariously through people we don't know, usually people who are famous in some way. Your Supporting Cast can also include people you don't know personally. For example, LeBron James is a part of Dr. Lennie's supporting cast. LeBron has had a great deal of influence on him. Your Supporting Cast doesn't have to be people you interact with daily; they can be individuals you see from afar and just analyze. You might learn about their habits and think, *They could be a part of my supporting cast that will help me become the person I need to be.* In this way, they can inspire you toward your goals.

Your Supporting Cast can also be people you know personally and either idolize or just look up to. Out of those people, you can identify mentors. In our work, as we move to the next level of what we are trying to do or who we want to become as Drama Doctors, it's clear that there are people who have retired from the field we work in who can still provide valuable insights.

For instance, one of our accountants, who is working with our nonprofit, is older than Dr. Lennie. When Dr. Lennie sits down to talk to him, he gives Dr. Lennie great advice and helps Dr. Lennie learn from his mistakes after many years as an accountant.

This man is about twenty years older than Dr. Lennie. When they have a meeting, Dr. Lennie knows he can't just go into his office for ten to fifteen minutes; he will be there for thirty or forty minutes because this man always has so much to share. He's that kind of guy. After these meetings, Dr. Lennie always comes away having learned something new.

He can always say, "Hey, Brock, what about this?" and Brock shares his experiences. He's been in the business a long time, and he'll say, "No, Dr. Lennie, you don't want to do this. You want to do that." Then, Dr. Lennie will go back and share the information with Dr. Carmen. Brock is definitely an example of a member of our supporting cast who is also a mentor.

NO SMALL PARTS

When you're in government or education, you encounter a rather big mix of personalities. It's great; it strengthens our work. We're not specialists in just one type of human. We specialize in all humans!

There's a saying in theater: There are no small parts. We need to value all the characters, regardless of how much we want them involved in our lives. Think of it as, "I am valuable, and you are valuable, but you can still be valuable far away from me."

One manager we worked with had an experience that helped him develop a new approach to the "no small parts" principle. This client hadn't realized that some people in his company needed to be recognized and rewarded in different ways from other people. He needed to diversify how he extended praise and find a way to show that all individuals in the organization were valued.

It's possible that more money wasn't the golden ticket that would motivate everyone across the board, and having the awareness that some people need more than money can shift leadership style in a more impactful direction for everyone.

If, as a leader, you don't take the time to really care about the human side of your team, their family lives, and backgrounds, some people might not want to work there. Sometimes, a boss will go for years not knowing anything about an employee's background, family, or personal life.

Some people in your organization may want their identity to be more than just their title and their salary. They need the workplace to be personalized a little bit more.

Find out what motivates different people in your company or on your team. What do they, as individuals, care most about? Money doesn't have to be the only thing that motivates everyone across the board, and having that awareness can help members of our supporting cast feel valued.

Just because we're all OK and everyone's role is essential and valuable doesn't mean we want all these characters in our lives. When we apply this to our personal and professional lives, it doesn't mean we want to be on the same stage in the same drama with everyone. Maybe you don't want to have to pick up the phone every time a particular person calls. We have to continue to ask o*urselves, Which characters do we move closer to, and which ones do we move away from?*

It actually makes you better at your job and better at finding relationships when you can say, "There are no small roles; you have value, but you're not in my play."

This concept aligns with blocking in the theater, the placement and position of characters as a product of their different emotions—be it fear, love, hate, or confusion. Characters move closer to each other when the feelings are good and farther away from those they don't trust.

During our financial crisis and rebuilding period, there was an individual who was in a position to help us. He was in a department where they gave out grants and resources, and he could have definitely helped us with some type of contract or work. But instead of doing that, he asked us if he could do a small job for us. We said yes, but because we couldn't pay him enough money, we ended up not working with him at all.

There have been some good things that this person has done for us as well, so even though we now realize we'll never see our relationship as a strong networking opportunity, we can spend time with him every so often and ask him how he is and make small talk. But that would be about all, and that's OK.

We have discovered that there are some individuals in our lives who, for whatever reason, measure our success with their success. If we are successful, then they're not successful. Sometimes, they will even do whatever they can to ensure we are not successful or will not support us with our success, and thus impede our progress.

It's not about being a victim; we are all just different people. Who will you go forward with, and who don't you want to be around? Accepting people as they are helps you identify your characters and decide whether you want them in your life or not.

Research indicates that the people we surround ourselves with play a crucial role in shaping our thoughts, behaviors, and overall mindset. In fact, studies suggest that we tend to become the average of the five individuals we spend the most time with. This means that the attitudes, habits, and qualities of those closest to us can significantly influence our own lives.

UNDERSTANDING INFLUENCE: POSITIVE VERSUS NEGATIVE

It's essential to recognize the type of influence the people in our lives have on us.

Positive influence: These are the individuals who inspire and uplift us. They motivate us to pursue our goals and dreams, challenge us to step out of our comfort zones, and support us in times of need. Positive influences can come from friends, family, mentors, or colleagues who encourage healthy habits, foster personal growth, and instill a sense of optimism. When we surround ourselves with people who embody these qualities, we are more likely to adopt similar positive behaviors and mindsets.

Negative influence: On the flip side, some individuals can drain our energy and limit our potential. Negative influences may include those who criticize us, undermine our efforts, or encourage destructive habits. These relationships can foster feelings of self-doubt and complacency, making it difficult for us to realize our full potential. It's important to be aware of such influences as they can lead us down a path of stagnation or regression.

You can use the following lists to evaluate your personal and professional circles:

KEY QUALITIES OF PEOPLE WHO UPLIFT AND SUPPORT YOUR GROWTH

- Empathy and emotional support
- Shared values and interests
- Growth mindset

- Respect for boundaries
- Trustworthiness and loyalty
- Nontoxicity

RED FLAGS—IDENTIFYING TOXIC RELATIONSHIPS

- Constant drama
- Jealousy and competition
- Disrespect or dismissal of your boundaries
- Gaslighting
- Lack of accountability

HOW TO ATTRACT THE RIGHT PEOPLE INTO YOUR LIFE

- Self-awareness
- Be the person you want to attract
- Expand your circle
- Set healthy boundaries
- Avoid negative influences

NURTURING HEALTHY RELATIONSHIPS INCLUDE

- Open communication
- Uplifting and supporting each other
- Empathy and emotional support
- Shared values and interests
- Growth mindset
- Respect for boundaries
- Trustworthiness and loyalty
- Nontoxicity

Depending on your motivation, you may not always be able to choose. You may have to put yourself around certain people and maintain those relationships. You may want to join certain clubs or organizations, attend certain functions, or do certain activities to spend more time with people who align with your interests and goals.

Identifying who the good actors are and who the bad actors are takes work. We have specific actions you can take in this direction in the "Create Your Best Role" section at the end of this chapter to get you started.

Once we identify them, how do we deal with bad actors in our careers and personal lives? Of course, it depends on the situation, but oftentimes, it simply comes down to proximity. Sometimes, we just need to stay away from someone.

For example, a councilperson in our area recently got into some trouble. He grew up in a bad community, and he was still hanging out with the same people from that neighborhood. To make a long story short, they charged him with bribery for taking money from one of the city contractors. Dr. Carmen pointed out that he needs to change his supporting cast. He should not be hanging around the same people he grew up with—he needs to be in a whole new environment to support his success and keep himself on the right track.

It's clear that we're talking about making choices here—choices about people we may even really enjoy being around sometimes, but who, for some reason or another, we realize are not in our best interest and are not aligned with our motivation. For instance, Dr. Lennie has friends who like to go out for drinks sometimes. He likes these people, but he's not going to hang out with them because, as we've discussed, he needs to get to bed early so he can get up early to work out, and besides, he doesn't drink.

For you to play your best leading role in your life, you need to be around people who have the same or similar motivations as you do. You need to take your social and professional relationships seriously in this way. Focus on how they will and will not align with your "why."

The choice is yours: Who will be your supporting actors and actresses, and who will not even be cast in your show?

In the film *As Good as It Gets*, Jack Nicholson's character, Melvin, says, "You make me want to be a better man" because he's had a very negative outlook for a very long time, and his relationship with Helen Hunt's character is helping him change for the better. He has decided that he definitely wants her in his supporting cast. Sometimes, this realization that someone will support you in positive ways, support your growth, and cheer you on along the way to becoming your best self requires vulnerability. It's a way to admit that another person has had a positive and meaningful impact on your life.

Had we met in DC, we probably would never have gotten together or gone out, and we definitely would not have gotten married. Stereotypes and discrimination could have gotten in the way. Dr. Carmen learned from a young age that all the guys from Southeast Washington, DC, were bad boys. They were what everyone called "no good."

Fortunately, we met later in life, while we were each pursuing our dreams in New York. Later, we both graduated together and received our advanced degrees from New York University. As time went on, we were able to build our relationship and our business at the same time. We are both so thankful that we chose each other as our supporting cast. We did this only because we could see that we were both trying to pursue something meaningful, that we both had dreams, and that we were both hard workers.

While it's vital to think about Your Supporting Cast and creating your support network to ensure those relationships are strong and enduring, we also need to work on how we handle conflict. Conflict is real, and it's going to happen, both internally and externally.

Embracing Your Given Circumstances, understanding Your Character Motivation, taking change One Beat at a Time, and working with Your Dramatic Conflict all lead to the next dramatic solution: learning to cultivate Your Supporting Cast so that the people in your life are all those who will support you in living your best life.

CREATE YOUR BEST ROLE

Act Five: Your Supporting Cast

Self-Reflection: Identifying Your Circle

Fill in the chart below with the names or role titles of the people in your life. The circles are the roles and the rectangles represent the messages sent between the two.

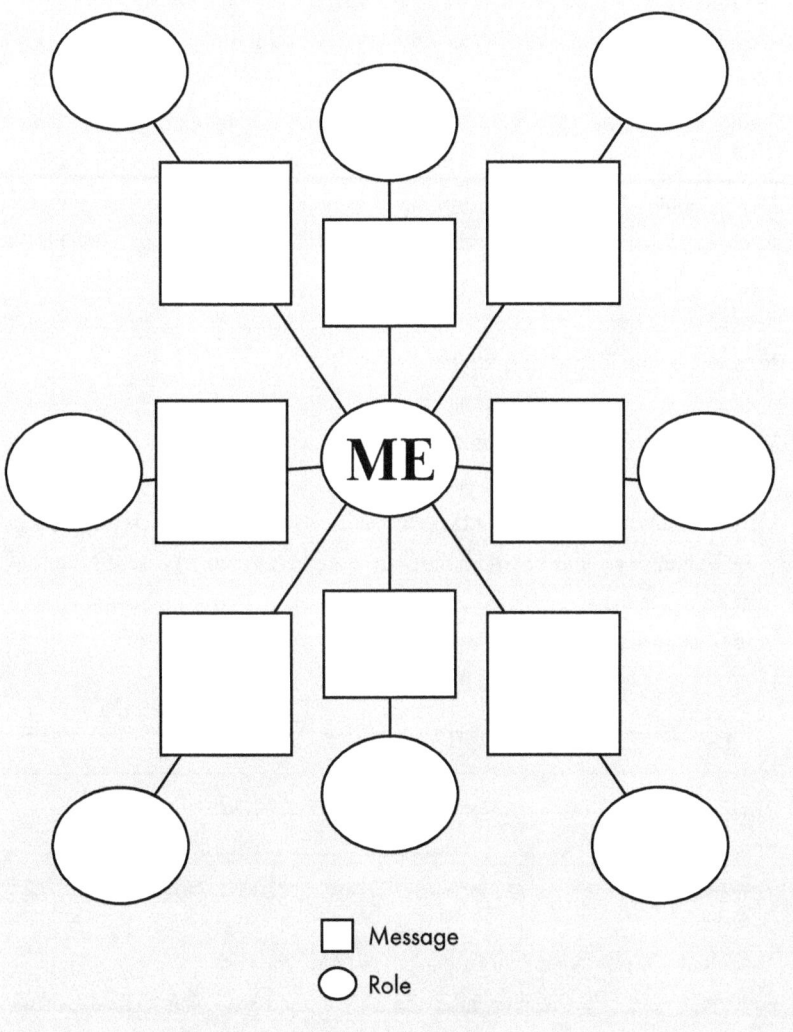

Take time to really think about the healthy voices of inspiration, guidance, and shared values versus the voices that may act as a judgment, hindrance, or negative indicator.

Identify those people whom you want to re-engage with more and preserve stronger bonds with others in your life. Perhaps you have identified relationships that need to be cleansed, hence create more distance in the relationship or just forgo the relationship at this season in your life. It is a central to give both yourself and others the opportunity to either massage the relationship in a healthy way and or invite an invitation to reset a relationship that's in need of repair.

Again, if you continue to have issues with people who tend not to be in direct alignment, just know that does not mean you must remove yourself from them forever simply because everyone wants to make shifts and operate from different spaces and convictions at different times in varying seasons of their lives.

Reflection: To better understand the impact of your social circle, take a moment to reflect on the following question:

Who are the five people I spend the most time with?

Consider how each of these individuals affects your life. Do they inspire you to be better, or do they leave you feeling drained and unmotivated? Jot down their names in the spaces below and take a moment to evaluate the nature of your relationships.

1. _____
2. _____
3. _____
4. _____
5. _____

After identifying these individuals, think about how you can cultivate relationships with those who offer positive influence and, if necessary, limit your exposure to those whose influence may be holding you back. Building a supportive network can lead to profound personal growth and fulfillment, empowering you to reach new heights in your life and endeavors. Remember, the people you choose to surround yourself with can have lasting effects on your path to success and happiness. Choose wisely!

ACT SIX

SETTING THE STAGE

"Do, or do not. There is no 'try.'"
—Yoda in *Star Wars: The Empire Strikes Back*

As we've shared, for years, we kept the fact that we were married a secret. We feared not making enough money or not being taken seriously enough because we were married, but at a certain point, we realized our being married had value as businesspeople.

We decided to honor the fact that we were husband and wife and stop hiding it. We began to acknowledge it more often. When people asked about our relationship, we would say yes, we are married, or bring it up more frequently. In the past, it had felt taboo, and we would jokingly say things like, "Don't ask us." We had become very comfortable with being uncomfortable about it.

Still, people noticed our chemistry, often saying things like, "You work so well together. You finish each other's sentences." We simply did the work that we had created together, but people looked at us and seemed curious. During training sessions, we can look at each other and know what the other is thinking. We are always one step ahead of each other and often know what the other is about to say.

Dr. Lennie might say, "Dr. Carmen, I need you to do a lecturette after this activity." She would respond, "Okay, I got it." We worked great as a team.

Surprisingly, we've realized that when people came to us and said, "I didn't think you were married," it was because we got along so well. "What are you talking about?" we would ask.

"It just doesn't seem like a marriage; I mean, you guys actually like each other!" they would say. It's sad but true; they really said that. People aren't used to married people getting along.

On the flip side, sometimes, when people learned we were married, it explained to them why we worked together so seamlessly. Every now and then, someone would say, "Oh, that's what it is. You're married; that's why." They'd remark, "I knew it was something." Of course, it was that, but it was also because we had been working so long together to build this program, so we were aligned on how to run our training sessions.

We had feared that people would somehow see us as a less powerful team because we were married. They might resent that we were both making money yet putting it into the same household. As if because we were married, we weren't allowed to stand alone as individuals. But we knew we each had our own educational loans, our own individuality. We needed to clarify that we were separate individuals even though we are joined in matrimony.

We even joked with people about how we ate off two different plates.

We had been keeping a secret, but we finally realized that it had value. We realized it was a strong commodity. Previously, we had feared sharing it because we didn't want to be seen as a minority company in a capital city. That would be shunned because everyone was trying to make a deal and get two for one. But we made it work for us. Dr. Carmen kept her last name. We retained our independent identities, and this was another way we were Setting the Stage. We visualized where we wanted to be and visualized a life after we'd made it happen. This was a big step in Setting the Stage for the next chapter in our lives.

IN ACTING

When Setting the Stage, an actor in the theater begins by asking questions like, "What can I learn about my character from the script?" This helps them identify the realities of who they are and their "given circumstances."

Secondly, they make decisions about who will be in the wings and what will be placed behind the scenes. The "wings" are where actors wait before it's their time to come on stage. In life, we can think of this as our safety net. We can assess what we have established to support us if anything goes wrong or if we are going through a rough spot. Who and what is waiting in your wings to help you?

Actors then sit down to prepare through deep reading of the script, exploring their character's motivations and traits.

Finally, they visualize themselves at the center of their own story, standing in the center of the stage with the spotlight beating down on them. They are wearing their character's favorite attire and best hairstyle and their character's shoes. They feel present and alive in the skin of their character.

You are the protagonist of your own story, and the best part is looking out into the audience and seeing yourself in the world, purposely prepared, protected, and moving into the promises you were created to experience. The lighting, ambiance, set design, sound, and props all correlate to how you set the stage in your home, your business, and your life.

When we finally decided to close the door on the franchise chapter and get back to our real work as entrepreneurs, one thing we realized was that we had to get out there and find our network and connect with the people who could support us as we rebuilt. This was our way of reestablishing ourselves and resetting our stage.

We began celebrating the people we knew were aligned with our goals, letting them know, "Hey, we have a lot to offer, and we want you to be a part of it." We maximized those relationships, and because we made that shift in our focus, opportunities presented themselves.

We stopped feeling bad about ourselves and got out there instead.

We shared what we were offering with whomever would listen. We needed their help, and we needed the work, but we geared the conversations more toward how we could help them instead of the other way around. Eventually, it paid off, and we were able to create new opportunities. This was one way we were Setting the Stage for our new life, but there were others.

THE MASK

We have found another activity to be profoundly useful when working with leaders in the school system—administrators and other education professionals, as well as deputy directors and directors of government agencies, and then their deputy managers and C-level managers. We sometimes help people with what we call "mask work" when we have the luxury of time, because it is a lengthy process. It can be hard for these high-level, extremely busy leaders to give up much time to really engage in this kind of hard work.

The mask work is based on perceptions: How do you perceive yourself? How are you perceived by others? The things you put inside the mask relate to how you want to be perceived by the world, while the outside of the mask reflects how others actually perceive you.

More specifically, the inside of the mask is based on your self-perceptions, while the outside faces outward—one side represents how you want to be perceived by society, and the other side shows how others see you. How do others form those perceptions? It's based on their prior experiences and prior knowledge.

This deep self-knowledge is not just for the sake of knowing about yourself. It is to be used for and applied to what you're doing now and how you lead others. Now, in this time and place, with the plots and themes you are currently living, how can you rewrite your story to let it inform your current circumstances? If you don't acknowledge those given circumstances, you may struggle to lead effectively. But this kind of reflection can help tune up your leadership skills so that the people you support and manage can feel more empowered, ultimately leading to more productive and higher performance outcomes. This can be a foundational element for Setting the Stage for your success.

WHY DELIVERY MATTERS: THE ART OF EFFECTIVE COMMUNICATION

Effective communication is an essential skill in both personal and professional spheres. While what we say is undeniably important, the delivery of those words plays an equally vital role in how our messages are received and understood. Research into the components of communication reveals fascinating insights about the significance of delivery.

According to the findings popularized by psychologist Albert Mehrabian, communication is broken down into three distinct elements:[8]

1. Verbal communication: This encompasses the actual words we use. While the content of our message matters, it is surprisingly just a fraction of the total impact. The language we choose can convey meaning, but it is only a small piece of the communication puzzle.
2. Tone and voice modulation: The way we say something—the tone of our voice, its inflection, volume, and rhythm—can significantly alter the interpretation of our words. For instance, a soft, warm tone can convey compassion and understanding, while a loud, harsh tone can communicate anger or frustration. Recognizing the power of tone is essential in delivering messages that resonate.
3. Body language and facial expressions: Perhaps the most compelling aspect of communication is nonverbal cues. Our posture, gestures, eye contact, and facial expressions can all send messages that may contradict or reinforce what we verbally articulate. For instance, crossed arms can imply defensiveness, while an open

---

[8] "Body Language, Voice & Words." Revolution Learning. Accessed August 6, 2025. https://www.revolutionlearning.co.uk/article/body-language-voice-words/.

and welcoming posture fosters engagement and trust. The human face alone can express a myriad of emotions—from joy and surprise to confusion and sadness—often conveying messages more powerfully than words alone.

THE NUANCES OF DELIVERY

Understanding the components of delivery is just the beginning. To communicate effectively, one must delve deeper into the nuances that accompany these elements.

Tone of voice: The expressiveness of our voice can make or break a message. Soft tones can create intimacy, while louder tones may be necessary to command attention or convey urgency. Varying your tone to match the context and purpose of your conversation enhances clarity and engagement. Enthusiastic delivery can inspire and motivate, while a bland, indifferent tone risks losing your audience's interest.

Body language: Nonverbal cues, including body posture and gestures, are critical to effective communication. An open posture invites dialogue and connection, while a closed posture may signal resistance or discomfort. Effective communicators are aware of their body language, consciously choosing gestures that complement their verbal messages. The use of eye contact is equally essential; too little can convey disinterest, while too much can feel invasive. Striking the right balance creates a comfortable space for interaction.

Facial expressions: Our faces are powerful communicators. They can express genuine emotions and reinforce what we are saying. A smile can convey warmth and friendliness, while a frown might indicate disagreement or unhappiness. Learning to align facial expressions with the tone of voice and the message being delivered will enhance authenticity in communication.

Pacing and pausing: The speed at which we speak significantly impacts understanding. Speaking too quickly can lead to confusion, while overly slow speech may create disinterest. Strategic pausing allows audiences to absorb information and gives emphasis to the points being made. Mastering the rhythm of your speech creates a more dynamic and impactful conversation.

Context: Context is critical in determining how communication should be delivered. Situational awareness allows us to tailor our messages according to our audience and environment. For example, delivering a speech in a formal setting differs vastly from having a casual conversation with friends. Understanding cultural nuances also plays a significant role in effective communication—what works in one culture may not hold true in another. Being adaptable and aware of the context can significantly influence how your message is received.

LISTENING SKILLS: THE OTHER HALF OF COMMUNICATION

Effective communication is as much about speaking as it is about listening. Active listening is the bedrock of meaningful interactions. This two-way process is not merely about hearing the spoken words but involves fully engaging with the speaker.

Techniques such as mirroring, reflecting, and paraphrasing can enhance understanding and show the speaker that their thoughts are valued.

- Mirroring involves subtly mimicking the speaker's body language and tone, creating a sense of rapport and connection.
- Reflecting allows the listener to summarize or echo what has been said, reinforcing the message and clarifying if any misunderstandings exist.
- Paraphrasing gives the speaker reassurance that their points are understood while also providing an opportunity to elaborate or clarify further.

In mastering these components of delivery, communication transcends mere words and becomes an art that fosters clarity, connection, and understanding. By appreciating the interplay of verbal and nonverbal cues and recognizing the importance of context and active listening, anyone can become a more effective communicator, ensuring their messages land with impact and authenticity.

In the following chapters, we will explore practical techniques and strategies for honing these skills, ensuring that your communication not only conveys the intended message but also establishes rapport and fosters deeper connections with your audience.

Dr. Lennie learned something about listening after running a meeting one time. After the meeting, Dr. Carmen asked, "Why did you run the meeting like that?"

And Dr. Lennie said, "What are you talking about?"

Dr. Carmen said, "You ran the meeting but wanted everyone to do what you told them to, but it seemed to me you weren't listening to them and finding out what they thought or what they needed."

Dr. Lennie realized that he had a certain preconceived notion in his mind. He thought that if others in the meeting weren't saying anything, especially when he opened up the room for comments or questions, then they didn't have anything to say. He realized he may have had a bias against people who might be a little more shy or passive and have difficulty speaking up.

His thinking was, *Well, I asked if anyone had anything to ask or say, and no one said anything, so whose problem was it if someone didn't feel like they were getting their needs met in the meeting?*

Dr. Carmen's point, though, is that if you don't make space for others who might be more shy or more apprehensive or who maybe have social anxiety, they might not speak up unless they're really given the space to do so. Some people really have trouble feeling safe speaking in public, whatever the reason may be. But they might have something valuable to contribute to the organization or your relationship. They might be part of Your Supporting Cast, and so if you want to really set the stage, then create an environment where everyone feels comfortable and valued.

TAKING STOCK TO SET THE STAGE

Part of Setting the Stage might involve levels of self-preservation. If something stresses you out and drains your energy, maybe you need to look at that and see how you can eliminate it. For example, as in Dr. Lennie's case, maybe you need to change your relationship with social media and watch less news so you don't get stressed out or overly anxious because of it.

Ironically, Setting the Stage for your future often involves reflecting and reexamining your past, really being reflective and reexamining your own history. Looking deeply behind the scenes at your own life and allowing yourself to accept things that have happened helps you gird yourself and gives you a platform for protection. Embracing your story to set your stage gives you an appreciation and the direction required to create the stage for your success.

You want to look at the past as a whole—the celebrations, the accomplishments, the missed opportunities, the weaknesses, the gaps, the hurt, the trauma, the recovery, and the rebound.

It's critical that as you prepare to set up your next stage in life that you consider the components of ones' attitude and behavior that influences you to thrive. Therefore, identify your dominant values that help you build and own your newfound space. Take a moment and ask yourself are you more of a Feeler, Thinker, and/or Doer in life? The simplicity and power of the Three Little Words by Leon Pomeroy, PhD, author of the paper, "Beyond Good and Evil," states that "Feeler, Doer, and Thinker" dimensions strongly influence all behavior and the construction of identity, personhood, self, and self-esteem.[9]

If you're a feeler, you're going to set up a different type of stage than if you're a doer or a thinker. If you're a thinker, you'll know you cannot live in a cluttered environment. You'll have a very organized space. You might stock up on candles and bubble baths and get massages if you are a feeler, because you'll be very sensory-oriented.

---

[9] Pomeroy, Leon. "Beyond Good and Evil: Are You a Feeler, Doer, or Thinker?" *Psychology Today*, August 29, 2015.

One way to gauge these differences is to notice what stresses you out. Dr. Lennie, for instance, is a conscientious thinker with a lot of opinions about things. He has to be around people he can debate with and educate as well be educated by.

Dr. Carmen enjoys downtime with many candles nearby, maybe a sweet treat, and definitely soft, fuzzy pillows. She also knows that the sound of water is very important to her. She needs peace and calm. A doer will need something else, depending on the things they like to do. If you are a doer, you'll set up your space based on your character type and fill it with, well, things to do. You can also think about your values and your strengths when you set up your space and choose the environments you will spend time in. Everyone is different and has different psychological needs. The important thing is to focus on ensuring that your space aligns with who you really are.

We are not saying that people are only one of these character types. We all have some doer, feeler, and thinker aspects in our makeup. But almost everyone has much stronger tendencies toward one of these than another. Usually, one of these traits is dominant.

In the next chapter, we will explore this in more depth as it relates to "acting as if." The whole issue of confidence and faking it until you make it can't be addressed until you have created the inner and outer environments for it.

Part of Setting the Stage for yourself is doing the heavy lifting that gets lighter every time you do it. By this, we mean getting very introspective, doing some deep self-examination, and really taking stock of your strengths and your weaknesses as well as your possibilities.

You can ask yourself questions that will help you understand where you are on the spectrum of feelers, thinkers, and doers. One question is whether you prefer solitude or are more comfortable in a crowd.

Dr. Lennie is a thinker. He perceives the world through thoughts. Dr. Carmen is a feeler—she perceives the world through emotions. You can probably recognize how the feeler-doer-thinker framework aligns with the three basic ways we perceive the world.

Midway through the summer of 2024, our business was overwhelmed with new clients. We had a lot of public school principals and administrators taking our professional development training.

We had to hustle and grow our resources to match the growth in our clientele. We decided to add materials to our work and take action to formalize a lot of what we are doing in manuals and training guides and those kinds of things.

At the end of the day, there will always be people who are in need of personal and professional development. They need guides, hints, or tips to become their best selves. Knowing this, Dr. Lennie decided to create our *Reflection Journal*, and it has been very well received.

One client accidentally left hers behind and then went out of her way to come back and retrieve it. Another asked for an extra one to give to her friend, who she thought would benefit from it. At one of the seminars we did for an agency in Washington, DC, with around seventy-five attendees, a young gentleman approached Dr. Lennie and said, "I hate to ask you this because I know you gave them all out, but is it possible that you have one more? Because I know someone who could really use this."

Setting the Stage is, first and foremost, exactly what it sounds like. You need to pay attention to the external and internal aspects of your life and how they set you up for success or not. Where you live, how you design and decorate your spaces, what you wear, how well you take care of your body and your physical appearance, and even what you drive all make up the stage on which you're going to live your best role. It's your desk, the rug, and the curtains or blinds. It's the lighting and the costumes and the makeup, as well as the props—it's everything that sets the stage so you can perform at your very best.

If you're going to become a lawyer, make sure you have suits. If you want to be a basketball player, your physical space should surround you with athletic equipment and inspiration. If you're going to sell things door to door, make sure you have good shoes and a reliable car. Once you identify what role you're going to take on, you must make sure your space and possessions are arranged to support the character you're going to portray.

Those are some external ways we can set the stage. But there are also internal ways we need to do this.

We strongly believe in the value of Studying Your Craft as a way to prepare for your best role. This can be as simple as taking a course or watching a YouTube video to learn something you need to know. The important thing is to prioritize your training and development on both the personal and professional levels of your life.

One night many years ago, Dr. Lennie was working at a burrito shop when a man called about five minutes before they were supposed to close. He begged Dr. Lennie and the burrito restaurant to stay open. "I really want some burritos. I'll be right there," he said. Dr. Lennie agreed and said something like, "Okay, we'll stay open, just come on down." This man took a cab over right away, walked into the restaurant, and smiled. Dr. Lennie was stunned for a moment, realizing the man was Judge Reinhold, the actor famous for his role in *Beverly Hills Cop*. Dr. Lennie was in awe. He said, "Wait, I know who you are." He told Judge Reinhold that he was a young actor aspiring to make it big and asked him, "What advice would you give me?"

Dr. Lennie will never forget what the star said: "The ones who have longevity are the ones who train."

Role-playing helps one develop an ideal role from the inside out. If you have an important meeting or interview, a rehearsal, or are just meeting with someone you want to be closer to, you might want to find someone to role-play that with you so that you can rehearse your lines for the meeting.

If you're trying to get a particular job, find out who the first line of interviewing will be with and grab a friend or get on a call or Zoom with them. Play the interview or meeting out. If you can't find anyone to engage in this with you, then you can become the interviewer and the candidate, stand in front of a mirror, and throw the questions out to yourself. Role-playing scenarios will strengthen your presence, your actions, your emotions, and your thoughts when it comes time to actually take the stage and play your best role.

If you can step into the shoes of someone you're going to be talking with and someone you perceive to be helpful in reaching your next level of success, role-playing can be a great strategy.

THE STAGE WITHIN US

The stage we are setting to perform our best role isn't just our physical appearance and our environment. It's not only the objects and set dressings but also our mindset and emotional well-being, our character, and our aptitude for the actions we are going to take. Often, it includes another theatrical term: Study Your Craft. Perhaps you need to go back to school, take a course, or just do some reading and research in certain areas to play your best role. It's both the space around you and the internal awareness of who you are and how you may need to grow in the future.

We want to incorporate all the senses as we prepare—the smells, sounds, sights, tastes, and feelings, and even our sixth sense, which we can access by listening to our inner voice and intuition.

Some aspects of Setting the Stage are both external and internal. To become really good in your role, you have to make sure that your body is physically prepared and you are mentally focused. This can mean doing breathing exercises, mindfulness activities, and physical exercise to release stress, build focus, and develop your strength. When you're ready to take on the character and perform, you've completed all these internal exercises. Doing this frees you up mentally to listen and portray that character because, as an actor, you have to be in the moment and present.

MIND, BODY, AND SPIRIT

You have to create an environment that supports your goals in every way, and this includes what you choose to eat and drink.

You may realize that you need to go to sleep earlier. Just like Dr. Lennie, if you want to get up early and have time to work out to get into better shape, you have to work on getting to bed earlier. Have your gym stuff ready to go in the morning. You don't have to be an Olympic champion; you simply need to set the stage appropriately for your own definition of success.

We have a client who isn't passionate about his work environment anymore. He's a business manager for a school. We gave him this insight—we said, "It sounds like you're not working the job; the job is working you."

The difference is whether you're happy doing your job because you know it will work for you or not. It will get you somewhere, even if that means retirement. On the other hand, if the job is working you, you may have become a victim of your situation.

Waiters are a perfect example. The best ones do their job with a positive attitude and an interest in great service because they know they're just doing this until the real thing they want to do comes along. In the meantime, it is paying their bills. They're in school, or they're preparing in some other way for other endeavors. The not-so-great waiters are grumpy because they're unsure of what they want in life and might be stuck in a rut, and their service is usually not too tip-worthy.

The problem isn't the job; it's the lack of motivation. It's the lack of a proper mindset that sees that this job might not be the be-all and end-all, but it's helping you along on your path, and it's a means to an end. In that case, the stage that needs to be set is the inner work—you need to change how you see your job and consider it a stepping stone toward a higher level.

On the other hand, sometimes, when you're unhappy in your job, it's time to get out. For instance, we had a friend who applied for a higher position at her work and didn't get a promotion. She was really disappointed. But she didn't leave; instead, she's going up for a different promotion in the same company. But we wondered, if the company didn't see her worth the first time, and if she is not happy in that job, why is she still there, waiting around, hoping they will see her worth someday and give her a promotion? Sometimes, Setting the Stage means changing your entire workplace situation.

BAD ACTORS

When we were in the process of rebuilding our business in 2015 and 2016, we had to change the whole structure of our company. We had to move from the pity party of panic that we were feeling over the sudden downfall of our business to a mindset of celebrating our networking. We looked at other characters in our lives and evaluated how good they were for us. We looked at how we were taking care of ourselves and our bodies. But that wasn't all.

We had to mobilize all of the resources available to us and reach out to all of our existing connections, exploring the possibilities for getting new contracts and getting more work. We most certainly evaluated all the characters in our lives and made decisions about whether they were the good actors or the bad actors in our lives.

Do you have some "bad actors" in your life? We aren't always even aware that a bad actor in our life has turned into an unhealthy relationship. We don't realize how much energy we put in and how much it drains us. Until you have that aha moment and awaken to the bad relationship, you can't act on it and make a different choice to either keep them in your life and work with the situation, try to improve it, or let them go.

All this is part of Setting the Stage for success.

Here's a short list of things to think about when you're Setting the Stage:

- How can I create more good habits?
- How can I change my environment, my image, and my behaviors?
- How can I improve my mindset?

In *The Empire Strikes Back*, Yoda says, "Do or do not, there is no try," to stress how important it is to fully commit to a goal by taking action and by believing you can succeed. He was trying to help Luke focus on the here and now instead of worrying about the future. Instead of trying, which leaves room for doubt, we need to throw our whole selves into it with full conviction that we can achieve it. For example, let's say you are in a consulting or management profession, and you want to grow to a higher level in your business or career. To do that, you'll need to acquire new skills and develop new relationships. You'll need to assess whether you are dressing the part, acting the part, and embodying the role you are striving for. You also may need to do continual professional development to hone your craft and commit to constantly growing.

This is the perfect time to acknowledge things that took place behind the scenes in your past and to make preparations for what can potentially take place in the next chapter of your story. When we own prior knowledge, we are building a skill set to protect ourselves from making the same mistakes, repeating icky behaviors, and staying stuck in an unproductive mindset.

What if you are one of the many people who still aren't sure where you want to go in life or what your best role would be? It starts with your motivation. Get very clear on your "why," reflect on what is truly driving you, and let that guide you toward your more concrete objectives and your vision for the future.

Ultimately, your motivations drive many of your choices, such as the choice to leave a particular job. Remembering your "why" helps you keep moving forward. It acts as a North Star that anchors you.

We have already discussed the three levels of motivation. Making a list of each of the three levels of motivation involved in your goals can help you gain clarity around this. What are your wants? What are your needs? What are your must-haves? That is the groundwork. Once that groundwork is done, you can set the stage to live the life that will serve your motivations.

There are also things we are still doing now to continue setting our stage. One of the biggest areas in which this is happening is our health. We've started eating healthier and getting more exercise and rest. Our work can be very stressful and demanding, so we realized we needed to take more time out for ourselves, finding more mindful moments—a space to relax, relieve stress, and breathe.

Dr. Carmen has started meditating and going to Jazzercise and yoga classes. And, of course, Dr. Lennie is going to the gym most mornings. We have also created an environment in our home that allows us to nurture our bodies and spirits.

Visualization can help you create the look and feel of your stage in a powerful way. As an actor, you have to visualize yourself achieving your goals. You need to see it first. So, when working with our clients, we incorporate visualization exercises such as the ones in this book. We encourage people to see themselves in that house, doing that job, or living that life. When done properly, it never fails to help people identify where they want to be.

We talked about good actors and bad actors in the previous chapter, and that certainly ties into Setting the Stage for your success. This means looking at the characters and people in your life and making a hard assessment of how much they will support you in your best role.

If you are hoping to make more money, find a better job, or improve your relationship, for example, you'll want to look at the kind of people who will support that, either overtly or inadvertently.

Your stage needs to be a space that is so well set that it allows you to expand. It enables you to leave it and come back to it if needed. It's about tonality and preparation. What kind of feeling or vibration do you want and need in your environment?

Early in the rebuilding process, when we decided to go on ancestry.com, we were also starting to do some SWOT analysis, looking at our strengths, weaknesses, opportunities, and threats. In order for us to come up with a small analysis of ourselves, we had to look at our past and ask what we learned from our past that's going to give us the strength to move forward. What are some of the mistakes that we made that might make us a little weak? What are the opportunities that come from our past and present experiences when it comes to business and relationships? What are some of the things that could currently be considered threats?

We were also starting to look at our leadership styles. We asked ourselves why we were successful in doing certain things. Why were we not able to be successful at other things? Through this, we gained some new insight into how we deal with our employees. We discovered that we were running our business like a mom-and-pop shop. We were giving so much—taking them out to eat all the time, for example. When we acted in this way with one of our employees, they left unexpectedly, and we weren't able to get a return on our investment in that person. Another time, someone took the concepts and principles we use and left our company to start their own, using all of our materials. We weren't running our business as a business; we were running it as a family. And it hurt us. Taking a hard look at how we had operated in the past really made us change our systems and strategies.

Setting the Stage for Success is the perfect principle that allows you to look at what's happening in the wings, acknowledge things that took place behind the scenes, and give you a chance to make preparations so that they become clearer about what can potentially and ultimately take place in the next chapter of your story.

Being reflective of the past really gives you an appreciation and the energy required to create a stage for success by looking at the past as a whole: the celebrations, the accomplishments, the missed opportunities, the weaknesses, the gaps, the hurt, the trauma, the recovery, and the rebound.

Being reflective, reexamining the past, and looking deeply behind the scenes allows us to accept what is happening. We can then set up a platform for protection. We own our prior knowledge and build a skill set to protect ourselves from making the same mistakes again and again. We can stop repeating unhelpful behaviors and mindsets and acknowledge that we can put them in the past. Acceptance allows us to move toward a growth mindset as we prepare ourselves and set the stage for success.

Imagine how creative and empowering it would be to live in the center of your own story, standing in the center of your own stage with the best spotlight on you. You're wearing your favorite attire, sporting your best hairstyle, and feeling like you can be fully present in any moment of your life. You are the protagonist of your own story, and the best part is looking out into the audience and seeing yourself acknowledged and accepted by others in the world. You are purposely prepared and moving into the promises that you were created to keep.

You want your stage to be set, not so much to be perfect, but to allow you to have opportunities to stretch yourself. When the real world gives you some bad drama, you want to be able to bounce back more quickly. This is about your inner strength, your resilience, and your grit.

You are out there in the world, bad drama happens, and you are prepared. That, too, is part of Setting the Stage for Success. You have to have your safety measures in place. How can you build resilience?

You also have to protect your inner peace. Your brain and nervous system need to feel safe for you to be successful. This goes back to Maslow's hierarchy of needs. If you are worried about the roof over your head or the food on your table, you won't be able to work on improving any other areas of your life until those things are secured. Keep the body safe, the heart safe, and the brain safe. If our bodies, hearts, and minds don't feel safe and healthy, we won't feel good enough about ourselves, and we will miss those moments and opportunities.

Only when we build our confidence in ourselves enough through doing the work of Setting the Stage will we be ready for those once-in-a-lifetime external opportunities to step into the spotlight and be able to love every moment of it.

We set the stage to glow and grow and bathe in moments of opportunity for a full life. We set the stage to share our own light with the world through generosity, creativity, and all of our gifts.

It's hard to believe sometimes that we hid our marital status from our clients and much of the world for so long. But one of the most amazing things we've learned through our rebuilding process is how much creating an environment, identity, and mindset to encompass your best role as your whole self helps you get there.

Once all these things are in place, it's time to take the stage and play your best role. Set the stage for the great opportunities that are coming your way. Take the stage, stand in your own light, and give them a performance they'll never forget.

But first, the final principle to help you play your best role is to learn how to Act as If.

CREATE YOUR BEST ROLE

Act Six: Setting the Stage

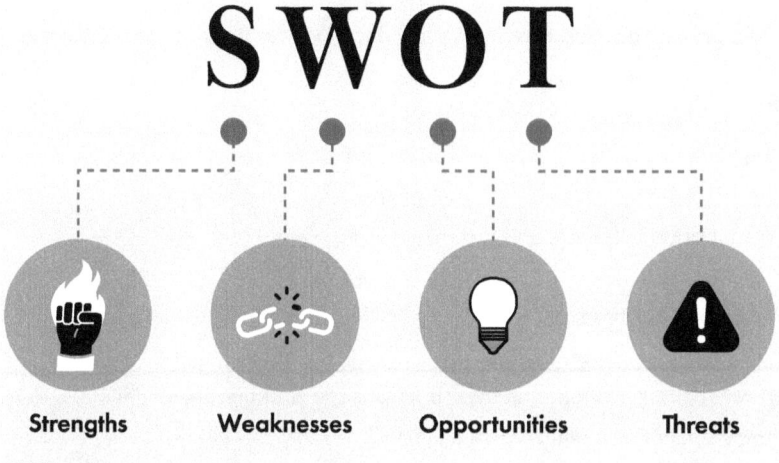

SWOT analysis

Do a SWOT Analysis:

Strengths: What are the core competencies and personal attributes that serve you? How do your strengths show up in your daily life or work?

Weaknesses: What areas do you feel you could improve as a leader?

Opportunities: What external opportunities (education, personal and professional development, relationships) are available to you right now as a leader?

Threats: What external factors (environmental, societal) are threatening your growth?

Questions for Reflection:

What are some pivotal moments in your life that shaped who you are as a leader?

How did you react to challenges and successes in your past?

What lessons have you learned from failures or setbacks as a leader?

Who or what has had the greatest influence on your personal or professional growth?

Are there any patterns in your weaknesses that you've noticed over time?

What opportunities are you currently missing out on, and why?

What external threats do you feel could derail your progress or growth?

How do your past experiences (both positive and negative) influence your present mindset or behavior as a leader?

Are there any recurring patterns you've noticed that you want to break or build on?

How can you use your strengths to overcome weaknesses or external threats?

ACT SEVEN

ACT AS IF

"If you build it, he will come."

—The Voice in *Field of Dreams*

We will never forget the moment we woke up in early 2015 and realized that everything seemed to be falling apart. We knew enough by that point to take some deep breaths and trust that we would figure it out. But there was something else we needed to do, and that was to get into the mindset of prosperity.

We both considered the possibility of getting a job. But deep down, we knew that was not what we were meant to do. We are entrepreneurs, so we had to wake up every day with the mindset of entrepreneurs. Neither one of us wanted to be stuck in a nine-to-five job, so we began the hard work of pursuing new and different kinds of contracts, and we kept believing we could maintain the lifestyle we wanted. We kept believing in ourselves.

We never lost sight of the fact that we are a very strong team and that we have the skills for this work. We had to let go of our condo in Florida, but we still retained the mindsets and behaviors of a couple who had that condo because we knew that this would lead to our ability to purchase in Florida again in the future. We just knew we had to Act as If we were a couple that still had all of those nice things. We used our imagination to put ourselves in the picture of the life we were putting back together.

When the time came, it was our "Act as If" mentality that helped us walk away from the franchise enterprise. In that situation, we both realized, "No, this is not who we are." This decision helped us return to the grind of getting things going with our own business again. Our Act as If mentality during this period also connected back to our supporting characters. Staying connected with the people in the world who were living the lives we wanted to live played a role in all of this as well.

It required a certain energy and mindset to keep pursuing that entrepreneurial path. We had to believe that we had everything we needed to make it happen. We kept the faith that we had everything to make it work, and we continued to believe in ourselves. It wasn't easy at times, but we knew it was the only way.

We continued to believe in our potential as motivational speakers and leaders. We focused on creating that energy and shifting our mindset to ensure we could continue living in our gift. That was very important.

To keep that energy high, we continued doing the things we'd always done. We couldn't afford big dinners at nice restaurants, but we discovered happy hours and could still enjoy some finer things at a price tag we could handle. We still went to Broadway shows from time to time; although maybe the seats weren't quite as front and center, we were there, and that was all that mattered. It's about putting yourself into those spaces and experiences to send the message to God, the Universe, whatever you believe in, that you belong there.

Continuing to go on short vacations and getaways, even though we'd lost our condo in Florida, helped us maintain that same lifestyle and still enjoy those experiences, but more importantly, it helped us stay in our mindset of prosperity.

As we discussed in Act Five, part of this is about surrounding yourself with people who are where you want to be, not necessarily where you currently are. So we worked on feeling comfortable and worthy of putting ourselves in spaces with people who knew more than we did. And we still do. That was and still is crucial.

Most importantly, we continued believing in our relationship. We had to continue believing we would make enough money again to feel comfortable, enough to pay our bills, take vacations, and enjoy a comfortable life. Shifting our mindset to feel free to live the life we wanted was also essential in providing for our children's education.

Remember, when all this happened, our kids were in high school, and when we lost so much, we didn't know if we could support them through college. We had to say to them, "You know what? We will keep preparing for your college expenses because you will be going to college." In that way, we "acted as if" we already had enough finances to support their college dreams. That was significant.

Feeling abundant and worthy was crucial for us. Even when we were going through a tough time and didn't have much, we still believed we could live the good life. We kept believing we could enjoy riches, even if it wasn't on the same scale as before. We had to start by doing it on a smaller scale, with the faith that we would return to a larger scale one day. By "rich life," we mean in all aspects: comfort, safety, love, peace, and spirituality. All those wonderful things make up a rich, worthwhile life.

IN ACTING

In the theater, actors have to prepare for their roles. They have to find their training wheels. This is also called "getting in character." This is the precursor to Acting as If. Performers engage with the dramatic techniques of getting in character in many ways, and one way they do that is through what Stanislavski called "The Magic If" and what is commonly known as acting as if.

Acting also teaches us to play different roles at different times. In the theater, we know that our characters always change depending on the stage we are on and the role we are playing. Acting as If is situational; the role you're playing can change minute to minute.

Jim Carrey was aware of the power of Acting as If. He is said to have written himself a check for ten thousand dollars while he was still living in his car and trying to become a working actor. He kept the check in his wallet for years, until one day, eventually, a check for that amount was placed into his hands after he was hired to star in *Dumb and Dumber*, and this "mind over matter" approach is what we will explore in this chapter.

IT'S ABOUT MINDSET

Once you have done the prework of reflection, activities, and visualizations outlined in the previous chapters to create your best role, you will want to carry yourself as if you're already playing it. You can simply shift your mindset to the mindset of someone who is playing this leading role. You are already there. If you've dreamed it up through intentional visualization, you can envision it and then decide you are already there.

The idea that your thoughts can change your reality is not new. The Law of Attraction asks us to decide that we are exactly where we envision ourselves to be. That is Acting as If you already are what you aspire to be. The idea is that if you manifest and affirm something and truly believe you have it, it comes to fruition. Dr. Carmen has always told people, "I'm exactly where I envision myself to be." This is the mindset of Acting as If, and it's also the technique used in manifestation. It's why we stress visualization so much in our work, and it's why we ask you to do the same.

One way to start is to communicate with others as if you have already accomplished these things.

Role-playing is another effective way to enhance your ability to Act as If. Work with a friend or partner to play the "role" of who you aspire to be. What does it feel like? How do you act? How do you speak? What does it feel like to be that person?

OUR EVER-CHANGING ROLES

Acting as If can be intimidating sometimes. It takes courage to decide that you are already where you want to be. And it's even more complex when you realize that you have multiple ideal roles, depending on where you are and who you're with at any given time.

In our lives, we operate in multiple spaces: our homes, our workplaces, our community, our circles of friends. When you are with one of these groups, you're trying to achieve certain results, even if it's just connection or relaxation. When you are with another group, in another setting, you'll be trying to achieve different results, such as performance or problem-solving. The ways that you Act as If will vary from place to place and situation to situation. There are times when it's appropriate to Act as If you are in the coziest home ever, and times to Act as If you are ready for the red carpet.

Even when you are in the privacy of your own home, you have a role to play. Usually, it's about relaxation, comfort, and a sense of safety. But it can also be the "best mom" role, or the "best dad" role, or the "responsible sister" role that you are aspiring to play. Every space we are in offers an opportunity to play our best role.

AUTHENTICITY

Just because we are using our imaginations and shifting our mindsets, it doesn't mean we can't also be authentic and true to ourselves. Ask yourself when you are moving into the mindset of your best self whether that self is still authentic to who you are. Is that mindset aligned with your values? Does it feel true to you and close to your heart?

Even when you are going through bad times, you can choose to believe that you are still living a rich life. A key to this strategy is to combat negative thoughts or what is sometimes called "stinky thinking." Change your mindset to a more positive and grateful one. There is almost always something to be grateful for if you put your mind to it.

Acknowledge what might be hindering you from being your best self. What do you know you should do but have been resisting? We believe that you can be anything that your God-given talents allow you to be if you do the work to acknowledge what's getting in your way. Think about what you might need to change in order for you to play your best role with utmost confidence.

There is always a risk that you may still adopt your old habits until you get it right. Just keep going. Put your costume on and allow it to help you feel good about yourself. Involve all your senses—smell, touch, sounds, sights, and tastes—and make choices throughout your day that reflect your mindset of abundance and success.

A lot of people have dreams, but they don't have the patience to go through the process. We call this "Big dreams with little workmanship." The shortcut isn't sustainable for most people personally or professionally, and often, people miss the opportunity to have grit on their journey to achieving their dreams. They find themselves stuck and don't know how they got to that point. Just consider this: LeBron James did not wake up one day and say, "I'm LeBron James, a leader in my field and an NBA champion." No, he worked day in and day out for years to become the superstar player that he is.

We referred to studying your craft as an element of Setting the Stage, but studying your craft also comes into play when you are Acting as If. You can't always just magically know what to do in a certain situation that you associate with playing your best role; often, you have to study it and learn new skills and techniques in order to effectively and authentically Act as If.

One sure way to grow in your knowledge of the craft is to work with mentors who've gone down the path you are setting out on. Find your mentors and lean into them. They will help you study your craft and learn by example. They are Your Supporting Cast. Tap into those people you look up to—people almost always want to help lift others up.

ALL THINGS ARE CREATED TWICE

In his book, *The 7 Habits of Highly Effective People*, Stephen Covey's second habit, "Begin with the End in Mind," asks us to use our imagination and the ability to envision in our mind what we cannot currently see with our own eyes. His idea that all things are created twice suggests that the first way to change yourself is to envision the change mentally, and the second action is to create it in the physical world. Just like a building is built on a blueprint, the physical enactment follows the mental imagining.

Covey also speaks of "The Circle of Influence." These are things within your control, like your attitude and behaviors. This means that we have the power to change our situations through shifts in attitude, and these lead to small changes in our behaviors.

If, after reading the previous six chapters and completing some of the Create Your Best Role exercises, you still aren't sure what your ideal self looks like or how they will show up in the world, try thinking about archetypes. Archetypes are categories of types of people—for instance, the helper archetype found in nurses and teachers, the warrior archetype found in military personnel, or the thinker archetype found in engineers and philosophers. Who is your archetype? Asking yourself this can help you clarify your vision of a future that is self-designed to suit your God-given talents and brought about through the effort you will put in to get there.

OUR INNER MONOLOGUE

One rule in the theater tells us that it's not always what you say; sometimes, it's what you're not saying that has the most meaning and impact. By saying this, we acknowledge that our thoughts are always "talking" to us. You can think of this as your inner monologue.

In our coursework and trainings, we often talk about a person's inner monologue. This is that voice in our head that is chattering all day long. Take a moment to think about it. What are you saying to yourself on a regular basis? What inner monologue are you carrying around that may not be serving you? It has been said that, "The way a man thinketh, so is he or she."[10] Our thoughts are powerful influencers of our emotions and actions. Are you staying mindful enough and aware enough to curate your thoughts in healthy ways, striving for positive, creative, and grateful mental activity?

Here are some questions for you to ask: What are you saying to yourself? What inner monologue are you maintaining? This introspective work is crucial for Acting as If. Are there voices saying, "You don't deserve this" or "You can't make it in this arena"? We challenge you to start listening for those diminishing inner voices. The way a person thinks is who they become.

The Acts that make up this book are all interconnected, and Acting as If is especially so. The practice of Acting as If requires awareness of Your Given Circumstances, and it is often your story that is preventing you from living in your gift. To live in your gift, you need to commit to not living in your trauma anymore. Only when you own your story can you live without your trauma running your life anymore, and then you can be in the place where you can Act as If. Because if your story isn't the invisible character in your script anymore—and isn't in charge of your inner monologue anymore—you'll have the freedom to play your best role.

Once you've done the work in Act One, you'll have the tools to keep your story and the trauma it may contain from interfering with your goals.

TAPPING INTO HIGHER POWERS

If you want to have more of a spiritual life, ask yourself what that might look like. Where do you want to be spiritually? In our spiritual lives, we attend a Baptist church every Sunday. We often see the miracle of "claiming it" amid the pews of our sanctuary. In the spiritual world, "claiming it" is saying out loud that something you are work-

---

10   *The Holy Bible.* Proverbs 23:7.

ing toward is already done. "I've paid off all my credit cards." "I have given birth to a healthy son." "I am building a successful business."

These kinds of announcements to the world help create a mindset shift in the person announcing them. You can literally rewire your brain by changing your thoughts and your words. Be sure you are clear on what you want before you claim it, however, because words are powerful and most likely you will get what you ask for whether you really wanted it or not!

We have learned that it is important to seek help in the process of becoming your best self and playing your best role. Make sure you don't do Acting as If alone. Tell a friend or loved one, and seek some professional guidance from a counselor or therapist or even your doctor. When you are envisioning your future self, you'll be alone with those thoughts and that's just fine. But once you are actually Acting as If, don't do it alone. Allow others to support you on your journey.

Keep listening to others, and keep measuring your growth. It's just as valuable to assess when you've done something right and acknowledge that as it is to be honest with yourself when you've gone down an unhelpful path. Always be mindful of your strengths and weaknesses alike. When you've done something right, acknowledge it. Look at your cup and notice how well you've been filling it up. Give yourself more grace. And remember, no one is an island.

If you believe in karma, you understand that what goes around comes around. Be mindful of what you are putting out in the world. If it is positive, supportive, and peaceful, you'll spread goodness and receive goodness in return.

As you walk through the world in the shoes of your best self, you will also naturally attract the right people—the ones who will be in your corner. You will be drawn to people who have like-minded talents and aspirations, and they will be drawn to you. This is yet another positive return on the investment of Acting as If.

BOUNDARIES

The greatest of all actors have a heightened sense of their own boundaries, or what we like to call our balance beam. They know when to turn the noise up and when to turn it down. How much can we take on? How much downtime and quiet do we need? How many people can we have in our lives? How little is too little, and how much is too much? Where is your sweet spot in terms of limits? What levels of effort in one direction or another lead to your best outcomes?

These are the questions that you should ask yourself. Otherwise, you might end up dreaming of playing your best role but lack the energy or focus to actually take on the physical and mental demands your best role might ask of you.

You've done all the work, now you have to walk the walk. Now you have to believe it. Now you have to live it, embrace it, acknowledge it, and accept that you've done everything that you could possibly do. Now, just be it.

Being it means being present with it. It is about affirming yourself. This is when you adopt the mindset and behaviors of the person that you aspire to be. What is the mindset of the person you want to be? What are the behaviors of the person you want to be?

In our case, some of our mindsets and behaviors include being kind to others and holding a peaceful, conflict-free perspective, working out and eating well, and working hard. We consider ourselves liberated, caring, and full of compassion. We are highly invested in creativity and know that we are vessels of God. These are our mindsets.

Dr. Carmen lives her life, speaks her words, and walks through the world each day, mindful to reflect these mindsets and behaviors. Dr. Lennie seeks meaningful conversation and ceaseless involvement in helping others. We are both always working to adopt positive intentions and be great parents to our children.

DRESS FOR SUCCESS

As the saying goes, it never hurts to dress for success. Our son recently went through the hiring process and landed a new job. Before his first day, we asked him, "What will you wear?" He said the firm told him it was business casual. We reminded him that if he wanted to get ahead, he needed to dress the part. Dress shoes make us feel fancier on the outside, yes, but also fancier on the inside. That is why it's always better to be overdressed than underdressed when you're in a professional setting. Dr. Carmen has some days that she won't wear flats; she just knows she needs to be in heels. It gives her the extra feeling of height and power she may need that day.

Dr. Lennie stays mindful about wearing a suit whenever it's appropriate. If you're an actor playing a role, you dress the part, and it helps you feel in character. Since we are all just playing our parts every day in our lives, it makes sense to keep our daily "costume" in mind. It may sound like a small thing, but it can have a large impact. You will act differently. Your posture will change, your alignment will change, and your gestures will change. This all helps you function at a higher level and embody that to the fullest. Your image might be presented to the world in subtle ways, but it can have a powerful impact.

Dr. Lennie recalls an old friend, Johnny Gill, who sang at one point with the band New Edition. When they were younger, Johnny had a thick gold chain, and he told Dr. Lennie it wasn't even real. He explained that performers must present themselves as if they have more than they do. It's this mindset that can lead to manifesting our dreams. Dr. Lennie also remembers that when they were growing up, Johnny (or Boogie as he was called) would tell everyone that he was going to be a star one day. He would ride around on his bicycle with a car steering wheel in his hand and wearing a suit. We thought he was crazy, but he was just acting as if he were already successful.

Johnny is doing well now, but back then, he really didn't have much to his name. Yet, he put on the garment of success. This idea of standing firm and acting as if he already had what he desired was powerful. It's about putting yourself in the position of success, doing things as if you are already successful.

CLAIMING IT

Acting as If is harder than it looks sometimes. It's changing your thought patterns and eliminating negative thinking. You need to tell yourself, *No, this isn't going to be challenging; I can make it happen*, even when the obstacles are, in truth, incredibly challenging. It's an opportunity to examine what kind of limiting or negative mindset is preventing you from achieving what you really want in life.

In some religious circles, it's called "claiming it": it's claiming that you are going to be OK, that you're going to be successful, that you're going to be happy. You have to say it as if it's already done, and then those things can develop in your life in their own way. It won't happen exactly like you think it will, but it will happen. You just have to believe it with all your heart and soul. That's the hard part.

If you are looking for a relationship, for instance, you might be having trouble finding someone because you don't truly believe you're worthy or simply because all you think about is how much you want that, instead of putting yourself in the headspace of already having a wonderful partner.

When you Act as If, magical things happen, and you begin attracting the people you need to meet, even those you probably didn't know you needed. You start to see things that help you come across things you should read. That's how the law of attraction works—it works because we're part of a larger fabric. The universe has our back—if we get clear on what we are aiming for and open up to it.

GRAVITATE TOWARD YOUR SUPPORTING CAST

While you're in the "Acting as If" phase, envisioning and pretending to be who you want to become, it's essential to surround yourself with supportive people. Ask for help, accept it, and then act on that help. Even in your "if" moments of envisioning what you want to be, start to become it. Keep practicing and rehearsing. Keep asking questions and keep listening. Be mindful of where you might allow pride and ego to get in your way.

Take the time to be brave and courageous enough to really let people in because many of them are there to support you. Constantly evaluate where you are on a successful, sustainable, safe, and sensational life trajectory, and then keep embodying your future self.

A long time ago, in the first few years of starting our business, we ran into someone who was a high official in the city government. They didn't hold a big position when we first met this person, but we had worked with their daughter years earlier, helping her with monologues and acting classes. Years later, she grew up and started college, and then she started to pursue her career.

Later on, when we had left school, received our degrees, and returned to the city, her father had an opening for a position in his company. He sat us down, intrigued and happy to see us, and we presented our proposal. He asked, "How much is this going to cost?" Dr. Lennie told him it would be three hundred dollars for a forty-five-minute session, and he chuckled. He laughed and started to close the paper, saying, "Oh no, that's just too much. No one's going to pay you that. No, no, no. No one is going to pay you that anytime soon."

We have probably tripled that rate for a forty-five-minute session now. This illustrates that when Dr. Lennie quoted the man three hundred dollars an hour many, many moons ago, he was acting as if his numbers were going to stick. Eventually, they did, and then some. It also illustrates the importance of Your Supporting Cast being truly supportive of your dreams and goals.

Good drama is all about using these Seven Acts to create and play our best roles in life. Now that you've created your best role and taken all the steps leading up to this Act, you are ready to put yourself in the mindset of who this leading role is and to be already there.

One way to think of it is to hold your vision of your best role in your mind and then just be present with it. Affirm yourself in it. Acknowledge that you can step out there on faith and that you have the right to exist in this new way.

You can pretend to be whoever you want to be while being mindful of your strengths, weaknesses, stretch points, and limitations. And you should approach it all with a great sense of humility.

So, how do we adopt that mindset and behavior? We can simply Act as If we've already achieved those goals. We're already successful if we believe we are. Dr. Carmen envisions her best role as being at peace, conflict-free, but knowing she has all the tools to deal with the drama, both good and bad, that will come and go. She knows her best mindset is liberated and caring, full of compassion. Her best self is highly involved in creativity and recognizing that she's a vessel of God.

Because she knows this, she lives her life connected spiritually. She speaks, walks, and thinks with positive intentions. By living this way, she can be empathetic and be a great mom, a great wife, a great daughter, and a strong, empowered leader.

Most everyone is familiar with the quote from *Field of Dreams*, which is often mistakenly quoted as "If You Build it, They Will Come" (It is actually "If You Build it, He Will Come"). In the film, it was referring to Kevin Costner's character Ray's decision to transform his cornfield into a baseball field so that the ghosts of baseball players from the past could play one more time and fulfill their long-held dreams. The meaning of this that was adopted by our culture is the idea that if we create the mindset and the environment for the things or the life we want, those things or that life will show up. The concept of Acting as If relates to this: if you choose to embody the person you envision yourself to be once you are living your best life, you naturally will create that life. Create the field, and the players will come to play their best game.

When Dr. Lennie was a kid, about eighteen, even though he wasn't one to read a lot, for some reason, somehow, he came across M. Scott Peck's *The Road Less Traveled*. What he liked about it was its focus on spirituality and how it helped people examine where they wanted to be spiritually, physically, and mentally.

One time, he was working at a conference as a projectionist, and they assigned him to a particular room where someone was giving a presentation. He was in charge of the slide show—an early version of a PowerPoint. He was working on displaying the information to the audience, and then he realized, "Wait a minute, I know this information."

At the end of his shift, he asked his boss, "What's the name of this book? I read that book." His boss took him up on stage and introduced him to Scott Peck, saying, "I want you to know that this young man read your book."

Dr. Lennie was so young at the time that he didn't even think to ask, "Can I get a book signed?" He wasn't thinking like that. But he and Scott Peck had a short conversation. It was a long time ago, but he'll never forget it because he was just starting to read self-help books, and that was one of his first. It really changed his life. It got him thinking about where he wanted to be spiritually, physically, and mentally.

In a way, this was an early example in Dr. Lennie's life of Acting as If. He had read the book and gotten himself in the mindset, and then he was suddenly and unexpectedly in the room with the author. It's not about magic or anything supernatural. It's a law; there's a logical reason behind it. When you're in the space where you're ready to receive things, they're more likely to come your way. When you're prepared, opportunity knocks. That is why we set the stage. Once you set the stage, you're ready for your vision of your best role to become your reality.

In the journey toward personal success and fulfillment, one of the most transformative concepts is the idea of Acting as If. This powerful mindset enables you to cultivate the qualities and success you dream of. By embodying the traits of our ideal selves, we not only enhance our confidence but also reshape our self-perception, which in turn influences our reality.

THE CONNECTION BETWEEN OUR THOUGHTS AND OUR REALITY

Our thoughts, behaviors, and beliefs shape our reality in profound ways. This interplay is essential to understand if we are to harness our full potential. Cognitive behavioral therapy (CBT) supports this principle by illustrating how our thoughts influence our actions. According to CBT, when we modify our thought patterns, we can alter our behaviors and, ultimately, the outcomes we experience in our lives.

The trajectory of our lives can often be traced back to the narratives we tell ourselves. If we continuously affirm negative beliefs, we create a self-fulfilling prophecy that limits our potential. Conversely, when we adopt empowering beliefs about ourselves and our capabilities, we open the door to new possibilities and achievements.

Central to Acting as If is the transformation of our self-image. Confidence acts as a catalyst for taking bold steps toward our goals; it fuels our motivation and resilience in the face of obstacles. When we visualize and embody the qualities we admire in others or wish to develop within ourselves, we begin to make choices and take actions that align with that envisioned identity.

The psychology behind Acting as If suggests that our internal landscape creates our external reality. By believing we are already the person capable of achieving our goals, our actions will naturally align with that belief. This fundamental aspect of self-perception is crucial; it dictates not just how we view ourselves but also how others perceive us.

The "Law of Attraction" takes this concept further by asserting that our mindset can actively shape our reality. This theory suggests that by focusing on positive thoughts and visualizations, we can attract corresponding circumstances into our lives. Mindset shifts, therefore, play a pivotal role in creating tangible outcomes. By aligning our thoughts with our desired outcomes, we cultivate an environment where success can flourish.

One scientific underpinning for these ideas is neuroplasticity—

the brain's remarkable ability to reorganize itself by forming new neural connections throughout life. Our experiences and choices actively shape our brains. When we adopt empowering beliefs and behaviors, we literally wire our brains to respond in ways that are conducive to growth and success. This understanding empowers us to become our best selves.

Our self-perception not only shapes how we view ourselves but also creates our external reality. If you believe you are already the person who can achieve your goals, your actions will reflect that belief.

IDENTIFYING YOUR IDEAL SELF

A critical step in this process involves identifying your ideal self. This exercise requires introspection and honesty. Ask yourself: *What qualities do I wish to embody?* Perhaps you desire to be more confident, healthier, more successful, or better organized. Start by writing down these qualities, allowing them to serve as a guide for your transformation.

Once you have outlined the attributes of your ideal self, delve deeper. Identify the behaviors, habits, and thought patterns that embody that ideal. For instance, if you aspire to be more organized, consider the daily routines and practices that successful, organized individuals may engage in. By adopting these behaviors, you begin to reshape your identity and foster the confidence necessary for growth.

Building confidence and resilience and having a growth mindset are crucial to sustaining momentum on your journey. Embracing a growth mindset is a powerful approach that encourages the understanding that skills and success are forged over time through effort and perseverance. Instead of viewing challenges as roadblocks, those with a growth mindset see them as opportunities for growth and learning.

As you navigate the path toward your ideal self, remember that confidence is not an innate trait but a skill that can be developed through practice. Each step you take toward embodying the qualities you desire strengthens your belief in yourself, contributing to a more resilient and empowered version of *you*.

When you're doing the song and dance in whatever field you're in, Act as If you're the best in the world at it. Try "pretending" that you're living your best life. Pretend that you're 170 pounds when you know you're 270 pounds because, eventually, you're going to get there. Whatever the pretense is, it's invaluable to believe, and not just to believe, but to Act as If.

With our limited time on this earth, can we allow ourselves to be part of our own manifestations? We have a little bit of control over that variable. That's what makes the drama: the unexpected, the emotional ride, the highs and the lows. We think that makes for a good life, and because we've lived it, we know that Good Drama makes for a good life.

When we were figuring out what to do about our financial collapse in 2015, we discussed the possibility of us both getting jobs to help pay the bills. But we knew deep down we were entrepreneurs, and so instead, we dedicated ourselves to Acting as If we were already successful in our entrepreneurship. Of course, we had to do the work, too. We were diligent in putting ourselves out there, pursuing more and more contracts and going after different kinds of contracts to diversify our income streams. But it was the mindset and the behaviors that sprang from it that truly made it happen.

In our own lives during our emergence from the crisis in 2015, we most certainly Acted as If to reset our business and our lives. This notion was central to our journey. We were inspired by Stanislavski's teachings about acting as if, as well as our experiences as actors. Once again, the fundamentals of acting shaped our approach.

Once you've done your studying and research—your character development, as we call it in the theater—then you can congratulate yourself. You've done the work and the preparation, and now you are ready to put yourself in the shoes, literally and figuratively, of your best role! Just be it! Be present, and affirm yourself again and again as you step out onto the stage of your life and play the role. Do it on faith, and with the knowledge that you have the right to not just exist but also to thrive at the highest, most beautiful level God has intended for you.

CREATE YOUR BEST ROLE

Act Seven: Act as If

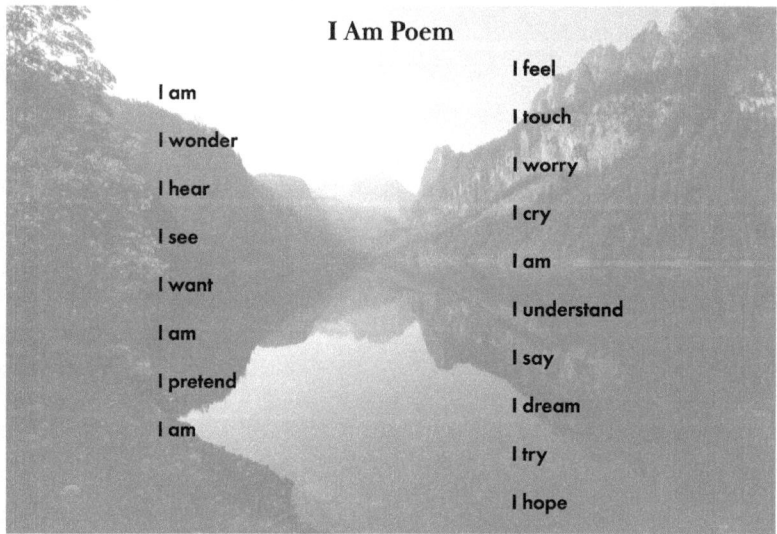

"I Am" poem

Action: We highly recommend you create your own "I Am" poem full of self-affirmations that will help you Act as If in your daily life. This exercise is about living, being, and doing things in the way you see yourself living, being, and doing them.

Imagine your outer appearance: your clothing, shoes, hair, makeup, body alignment, walking posture, disposition, as well as your potential responses to others.

Imagine that you are Acting as If. How do others respond and react to you as you boldly take center stage and humbly stand in your spotlight, glowing and enjoying every moment?

Now, make a list of all the things you are and all the great things you do.

From that list, create affirmations for yourself to repeat to yourself often.

Activity: Write an "I Am" poem. An "I Am" poem is a way to study the subject of a self-portrait by putting yourself in the artist's head.[11]

I am...(your name)

I am...(two special traits or physical characteristics)

I wonder...(something to be curious about)

I hear...(an imaginary sound)

I see...(an imaginary sight)

I want...(an actual desire)

I am...(the first line of the poem repeated)

I pretend...(something to imagine)

I feel...(a feeling about something imaginary)

I touch...(an imaginary touch)

I worry...(something that is bothersome)

I cry because...(something that is very sad)

I am...(the first line of the poem repeated)

I understand...(something that is positively true)

---

[11] National Gallery of Art. "I Am Poem." Education Resources. Accessed August 6, 2025. https://www.nga.gov/content/dam/ngaweb/Education/learning-resources/lessons-activities/self-portraits/i-am-poem.pdf.

I say...(something to believe in)

I dream...(something to dream about)

I try...(something to make an effort about)

I hope...(something to hope for)

I am...(the first line of the poem repeated)

For support and a deeper experience of completing this exercise or any others in this book, contact us about our trainings and other programs at dramadoctors@gmail.com.

CONCLUSION

IT'S ALL GOOD

You can't completely set the stage until you've embraced Your Given Circumstances. You can't identify your supporting characters without being clear on your motivations. The lines between the Seven Acts we present in this book will never be completely rigid. Everything connects. Choosing Your Supporting Cast sometimes requires you to take things One Beat at a Time. It's not necessarily a chronological, step-by-step process; the Acts are interdependent, and the path is circular.

We are grateful to you, the reader, for taking the time to read or listen and absorb these Seven Acts, which have helped us make a major reset in our lives and can help you do the same. We believe fiercely that Good Drama is a powerful tool for growth, learning, and improvement. By managing emotions and embracing healthy, constructive disagreements, individuals and teams can grow personally, strengthen their relationships, foster creativity, and solve problems more effectively.

It's NOT the drama itself that's important, but HOW it's handled.

When approached with understanding, respect, a focus on solutions, and open communication, drama can drive positive change and lead to better outcomes for everyone involved. Leadership involves interacting with people, solving problems, and making decisions in dynamic environments. We hope this book will help you see how drama helps to simulate these situations in a controlled, safe environment, allowing participants to explore different approaches and learn from their experiences. The many trainings and programs that Dramatic Solutions offers can help you grow, expand, and thrive in your business and your life.

If you take away just one thing from reading this book, let it be this:

You can be anything your God-given talents allow you to be in your life. You can play your very best role in life every day if you do the work to acknowledge what's getting in your way.

We hope the concepts and Acts in this book will help you achieve a much higher level of fulfillment in your life. It's not just about leadership effectiveness. This is about living your best life by creating your best role and then going out and playing it.

The ideas presented here are intended to help you boost self-awareness and self-management so you bring those aspects of your character to the table as an asset in your personal and professional roles. Improving your ability to manage your emotions, acknowledging Your Given Circumstances, and resolving conflict with others is fundamental to your own success and the success of those around you.

The time is right for you to go out into the world and apply a suite of communication and motivation tools to create a more inclusive, productive, thriving, and safe work culture and personal life.

Our working definition of drama is "an exciting, emotional, or unexpected series of events or circumstances." It is not necessarily wrapped up in any tragedy or trouble; if there's no drama in your life, you're not fully living. The low vibration processing of your experiences as bad, negative, or otherwise weighted toward the unpleasant really does not compute well in the brain. Therefore, during these "high drama" times of crisis, the body and mind become stiff, stuck, less adaptable, and less agile. Some complex situations may even paralyze both the body and the mental state.

However, if we start to manage our filter with more intentionality and start to intake information, thoughts, feelings, opinions, and actions in a way that's full of positivity, nuanced with gratitude, and thirsty for human growth, now that's seeing the bad drama as Good Drama.

This can compel you to release the happy chemicals of the brain such as dopamine, serotonin, oxytocin, and endorphins, and we are then able to be transformed, healed, and run this incredible race of life with ease, openness, and faith.

So, bring on the drama! It's all good!

ACKNOWLEDGEMENTS

This work is a creative product of experiences, education, and enlightenment. It began with our experiences as performing artists and students at New York University. We are grateful for the support and wisdom of many people and for the transgenerational sources and roots of this wisdom.

We are also grateful for many students, friends, and colleagues at the Creative Arts Team, New York University, and Dramatic Solutions, Inc., and for thousands of adults, parents, youth, executives, teachers, and other clients who have tested this material and have given feedback and encouragement. The material and arrangement have slowly evolved and have imbued those who have been sincerely and deeply immersed in it with the conviction that the Seven Acts represent a holistic, integrated approach to personal and interpersonal effectiveness and that, more than in the individual habits themselves, the real key lies in the relationship among them and in how they are sequenced.

For the development and production of the book itself, we feel a deep sense of gratitude:

FROM DR. CARMEN AND DR. LENNIE

To our children, Layla and Linwood, whose love, laughter, and endless curiosity have been our greatest inspiration. This book is for both of you; we love the two of you with all of our hearts.

To our colleagues and clients: Your expertise and guidance have enriched our understanding and pushed us to grow. Whether through thought-provoking discussions or simply by offering your time and insights, you've made this book better and more meaningful. We are fortunate to work alongside such talented individuals who not only challenge us but also remind us of the importance of collaboration and shared vision.

To our amazing editor, Candace Read: Your meticulous eye and thoughtful guidance helped shape this book into something we are incredibly proud of. Your feedback was invaluable, and your belief in this story kept us going.

We are also extremely grateful for our publishing manager, Katie Lathrop, who gave us invaluable advice every step of the way and helped coordinate a smooth path to publication.

A special thanks to our cover designer, Sheila Parr, who perfectly captured the essence of this book with her incredible artwork. It was a joy to work with someone so talented.

To our accountant, Charles Myrick: Your inspiration and guidance have inspired our company to new heights and growth. We look forward to moving to the next chapter of our business.

FROM DR. CARMEN:

Hats off to the funniest and most thoughtful man I know—my soulmate and best friend—for being the wind beneath my wings. It's been super healing and empowering to write this book with you. Thank you for creating a life for me and our family that has allowed us to live an impossible dream.

To my amazing mom and dad, Dorothy and Carlton White, for

being super engaged, nurturing, compassionate disciplinarians and introducing me to God and the stage.

To my grandmother, Mimi Irene Smith, for her agape love and for instilling in me the importance of education; my Popeye, James Smith, for his strength and high work ethics; and my grandmother and grandfather Estell and Rudy White for modeling the beauty of family, spirit, entrepreneurship, and what it means to work hard.

To the godfather of Children's Theatre and founder of Howard University Children's Theatre Playmakers Repertoire Company, Kelsie Collie, for allowing me to be a part of your dreams and quality performances, and for believing in me.

To my first mentor, Dr. Linda Wharton-Boyd, for being an example of what it means to strive toward excellence and for demonstrating what it means to be a triple threat.

To my initial coaches, Harry Poe, David English, and Mitchell Patrick, for deepening my knowledge base and encouraging me to perfect my craft.

To those who inspired the dancer and human in me: Judith Jameson, Laverne Reed, Adrian Bolton, Kathy Smith, and Dwayne Murray. Thank you for all your gifts.

To my beautiful Delta Sigma Theta Sorority, Inc., sorors, especially my incredible line sisters, for their love, motivation, and support.

To Pia Sterling, Jeanette McCune, Jessica Dulay, and Dr. Renae Neely: Every time I asked for advice regarding content, marketing, or just assistance with connecting the dots, you all went above and beyond.

To my supporting cast, my best friends Corliss and Allison, and childhood friends and friends for life (Minyon Mangrum, Sheree Hamilton, Denise Daniels, Kimberly Smith, Trina Tanner, and Vernandi Richardson) for their faithfulness, loyalty, and kindness.

To the memory of my biological mom, Eunice Bonnie Ross, and father, Bernard Allen Fennell, for their resiliency and devotion to family, and to my newly found family who have embraced me since the day I met them in 2017.

FROM DR. LENNIE:

First and foremost, I would like to thank my wife for her endless support and encouragement. Without you, this book would never have been possible. Your love, patience, and understanding have been my anchor throughout life and through this entire collaborative process.

I would like to express my deepest gratitude to the memory of my incredible parents, whose unwavering love, support, and guidance have shaped me into the person I am today. To my mother: Thank you for your endless kindness, encouragement, and the strength you've shown in every aspect of my life. Your love and nurturing spirit continue to inspire me daily.

To my father: Your steadfast belief in me, your discipline, and your sense of humor have been a constant source of motivation. The lessons you've taught me, both directly and through your actions, will forever be a part of who I am.

To my sister Denise and all my siblings, who have been a constant source of laughter and support: Thank you for keeping me grounded and reminding me that there's more to life than words on a page.

To my friends, especially Irwin Bookhart, Michael Copper, Randy Johnson, and Charles Austin: Thank you for being my constant source of joy, inspiration, and perspective. Your belief in me, even when I doubted myself, has been invaluable. Each of you has helped shape not only this book but my life in ways words cannot fully capture.

I owe a debt of gratitude to the late Charles Williams, Reverend Edward Cole, Keith Smith, and Thandor Miller, whose mentorship and wisdom lit my path when the road ahead seemed unclear. Your guidance has influenced my life and writing in ways I can't fully express. To the teachers and writers who have inspired me: Your words have been a guiding light throughout this journey. Thank you for teaching me that stories have the power to connect, to heal, and to inspire.

Lastly, I must thank myself. For those moments when I doubted and almost gave up, you kept going. You proved that persistence and grit are sometimes the keys to success.

ABOUT THE AUTHORS

DR. CARMEN WHITE is a renowned motivational speaker, leadership coach, drama therapist, and business consultant with over twenty years of experience helping individuals and organizations unlock their full potential. Known for her dynamic presentations and transformative coaching techniques, Dr. Carmen has worked with top corporations, startups, nonprofits, and educational institutions to inspire lasting change and drive performance improvement. She is the co-founder of Dramatic Solutions, Inc., a firm dedicated to empowering leaders and teams to create sustainable growth through shifts in attitude, behavior, mindset, and strategic action. Dr. White's journey into motivational speaking and consulting began after she overcame significant personal challenges. After experiencing financial hardship and personal setbacks, she developed resilience and a deep determination to thrive in the face of adversity. This transformative journey led her to discover the power of mindset, goal-setting, and emotional intelligence—insights that became the foundation of her career. Inspired by her own experience, Dr. White now helps others harness these powerful tools to achieve their personal and professional success. Her mission is to help individuals and organizations break through barriers, unlock their potential, and create meaningful, sustainable change.

DR. LENNIE SMITH is a seasoned communication and consulting trainer with over twenty years of experience helping individuals and organizations enhance their interpersonal, organizational, and strategic communication skills. Dr. Lennie has established himself as a leading authority in business communication, coaching, and consulting. His expertise spans a wide range of industries, including corporate settings, nonprofits, government agencies, and educational institutions. Throughout his career, Dr. Smith has worked with executives, managers, teams, and professionals at all levels, guiding them toward more effective communication strategies that increase productivity, improve collaboration, and foster inclusive workplace environments. Known for his engaging, hands-on approach, Dr. Smith blends theoretical knowledge with practical applications to ensure lasting impact. He believes that effective communication goes beyond speaking clearly or writing well; it is about understanding human behavior, recognizing cultural nuances, leveraging emotional intelligence, and adapting messages to resonate with diverse audiences. Dr. Smith's holistic approach equips clients to communicate with clarity, empathy, and purpose, driving both individual and organizational success.

www.ingramcontent.com/pod-product-compliance
Lightning Source LLC
Chambersburg PA
CBHW060524080526
44586CB00012B/607